MSU-WEST PLAINS
GARNETT LIBRARY
WITHDRAWN
tt Library

150
Jobs
You Can Start
Today

D1048792

150 Jobs You Can Start Today

CREATIVE WAYS TO MAKE MONEY NOW

DEBORAH JACOBSON

BROADWAY BOOKS • NEW YORK

150 JOBS YOU CAN START TODAY. Copyright © 2003 by Deborah Jacobson.
All rights reserved. No part of this book may be reproduced or transmitted in
any form or by any means, electronic or mechanical, including photocopying,
recording, or by any information storage and retrieval system, without written
permission from the publisher. For information, address Broadway Books,
a division of Random House, Inc.

PRINTED IN THE UNITED STATES OF AMERICA

BROADWAY BOOKS and its logo, a letter B bisected on the diagonal, are
trademarks of Random House, Inc.

Visit our website at www.broadwaybooks.com

First edition published 2003

Book design by Helene Berinsky

Cataloging-in-Publication Data is on file with the Library of Congress.

ISBN 0-7679-1609-3

1 3 5 7 9 10 8 6 4 2

To the most supportive and encouraging family
anyone could hope to have

CONTENTS

3. That's Entertainment: THERE'S NO BUSINESS

4. Do the Locomotion: JOBS FOR PEOPLE WHO WANT TO KEEP ACTIVE

INTRODUCTION

This book is about finding work now.

If you feel stranded by the new economy and today's ruthless job market, if you are a parent who wants to work fewer hours in order to spend more time with your family, a student looking to pay your way through school, an artist needing financial support until your big break comes along, or one of the millions of Americans who need extra jobs simply to pay the bills and save for your children's education, this is the book that will help you. Inside, you'll find 150 ways to take charge of your career, start making money, and possibly open the door to a whole new level of professional success and personal fulfillment.

I wrote *Survival Jobs* in 1996 to reach out to the thousands of people who needed immediate and flexible ways to earn their livings. At the time I was pursuing an acting career in New York and Los Angeles and was in need of unconventional jobs that would pay a good salary and allow me to go on auditions and do theater work. Many of my friends were also creative types who needed time to pursue their craft, and we had mastered the art of thinking outside the box when it came to generating income. *Survival Jobs* profiled over one hundred of these little-known professions, and the response from readers was so overwhelming that I thought a new version of the book—one updated with additional jobs and new information to reflect the current job climate—was in order.

The best part about the jobs in this book is that many of them allow you to start working immediately to shape your own destiny. You don't have to wait for a position to open up at a company, you won't be at the mercy of recruiters, and you don't have to worry about competing with hundreds of other applicants for the same spot. These jobs allow you to take the skills you already possess and create your own opportunities. Through speaking at seminars and book events, I have found that often people don't realize that their innate talents, skills, and enthusiasms can be used to earn money. Many people already pet-sit for neighbors, paint houses, plan parties, build things, play musical instruments, take excellent photographs, sing, have a flair for design, are great with children, or are computer-savvy. Believe it or not, these skills can translate into real dollars with a little ingenuity and guidance from this book, and they can ultimately prove quite profitable.

Over the years I have held a number of the jobs included here. When I attended college, I worked part-time in the evening, on weekends, and during summer months. When I became a mother, I used my skills and a few of these ideas to create part-time work that enabled me to earn full-time income right out of my home. But while much has changed in my own life since I first wrote *Survival Jobs*, what hasn't changed is my desire to help people find jobs that fit with their current circumstances and allow them to make money while pursuing what really matters to them. If you are between jobs, the options in this book can help you pay the bills while you look for work in your chosen profession. If you've decided that a graduate degree is what you need to get ahead, you'll find plenty of jobs in these pages that will see you through the application process and, if you choose, your years of schooling. Above all, you'll be in control. What's more, you never know, one of the jobs in this book may help you launch an entirely new career. One of my own survival jobs, Varied Musical Work (see page 121), evolved into my wonderful, now full-time career as a cantor (a spiritual leader and singer of musical liturgy in the Jewish religion) at a prestigious synagogue in Stamford, Connecticut. So the jobs in this book need not serve only as a Band-Aid; they can evolve into a much greater solution.

When I first wrote *Survival Jobs*, our economy was on the upswing. Today it's no secret that our economy has changed, and in most professions, jobs are harder to come by than ever before. We also can no longer rely on the stock market to provide us with a financial cushion to bridge the gap between jobs or pay for our children's educations. My hope is that this book will ease your burden by inspiring you with many interesting and unconventional ways to boost your income, pursue your dreams, and guide you to abundant prosperity in all areas of your life. I wish you every success.

1

You're the Top

JOBS FOR THE CEO IN YOU

Apartment Manager

If you never thought it was possible to stay home, eat potato chips, watch TV, and get paid for it, guess again.

Being an apartment manager is perfect for couch potatoes, writers, artists, moms, seniors, or anyone who stays home a lot. Some building owners will even hire people who already have nine-to-five jobs as long as they carry beepers. I know many couples who worked as apartment managers for a number of years to save for down payments on homes. What a great idea!

Basically, an apartment manager is responsible for collecting rent, keeping the building and surrounding area clean, and knowing whom to call in an emergency. Some positions may even require light maintenance. The actual labor involved in this job will depend on your tenants and the size and quality of the complex. Most large complexes (over fifty to seventy-five units) have special maintenance crews. Typically a ten- to twenty-unit building is easiest to handle. Some building owners prefer couples, but this is not a requirement. The main attributes that apartment owners generally look for are honesty, common sense, good credit, stability, and an ability to fill vacancies.

Most large cities have apartment associations that offer certified resident manager training courses. For example, the Apartment Association of Greater Los Angeles offers a training course approximately twelve times a year. It costs between $450 and $500, and the placement rate is around 80 percent. After completing the course, you can place an ad in the Apartment Association's employment bulletin, an excellent way to get a job. Most courses are extremely informative and well respected among apartment building owners. Another option is to explore a course that is subsidized by the government in your city. Many community colleges will offer an apartment management course for a nominal fee. You can also try calling the local chamber of commerce regarding an apartment managing course.

Whether you receive free rent and utilities plus salary will depend on the building you are managing. Smaller units often offer only a rent reduction or free rent, while larger buildings pay a weekly salary as well. This is often negotiable depending on your experience. Some management companies even offer health benefits and profit sharing.

To find an apartment manager position, check the classified section of your newspaper, contact building owners and management firms directly, and network with other apartment managers. You will need to submit a current résumé and a list of references. Also helpful is the *Encyclopedia of Associations*, which can be found at your local library: one for national associations and several volumes for different regions. The National Association of Residential Property Managers has local chapters in many states, and the National Apartment Association is in Washington, D.C.

Good luck.

- **BENEFITS:** Salary plus free rent and utilities or rent reduction; sometimes profit sharing and health benefits.

- **PITFALLS:** Overbearing owners and tenants; calls at all hours.
- **SOURCES:** Classified sections of newspapers. Apartment Association of Greater Los Angeles, 213-384-4131, www.aagla.org. Los Angeles City College Community Services, 323-669-1031, www.lacitycollege.edu/comsvcs. National Association of Residential Property Managers, 800-782-3452, www.narpm.org. National Apartment Association, 703-518-6141, www.naahq.org. Building owners and management firms.
- **NEEDS:** Prior experience; good credit; some basic maintenance ability.

Designing Greeting Cards and Postcards

The gift card industry is a thriving business. The average person receives about thirty cards a year. A neighborhood post office recently estimated that a third of all first-class mail consists of greeting cards. If you possess photographic, writing, or artistic abilities, you can become part of this booming industry.

Designing cards allows you to be creative and work at home on your own time. It also provides the excitement of seeing your work displayed. To be successful, marketing abilities are a must. If marketing is not your forte, consider hiring someone to help out.

You can turn anything into a postcard or gift card. I have seen beautiful cards with dried flower designs, twigs, and original artwork. Explore your designs, reproduce them, and test them out. To get started, go to an art store, library, or bookstore, and get a few books on card making; these can be found in the art technique section. The creative process comes next. If you are drawing or painting your cards, first draw a rough sketch, and then finish it in pen and ink. To save some money, go to a paper supply company that sells different kinds of paper whole-sale. Such companies often can be found in industrial areas.

Next, you can silk-screen your design or go to a copy center and laser print the sketches. You can then paint the prints with dry pigments, pastel sticks, or other media. After coloring your cards, spray them with an acrylic paint for protection.

Marketing your prototypes is the next step, and there are many ways to go about doing this. Visit a variety of stores and gift shops with your portfolio, and meet with the card buyer. You may need to make an appointment, but oftentimes, if you have a professional and courteous manner, you can just walk in and be seen. Many small stores and specialty shops buy their cards from independent artists. If a store is interested, it will typically order a small amount first and pay you upon delivery. Another good way to sell your work is at craft bazaars and flea markets (see "Swap Meets and Flea Markets" in this chapter). You can find out about these through friends and newspapers and by networking with craftspeople.

You can also sell your designs through card distributors. They will buy the rights and produce the cards. To locate a distributor that is right for you, go to a store and see which cards are similar to yours. Look at the back of the card to see what company produces it, and write directly to the distributor or manufacturer, requesting its market list, catalog, and submission guidelines. Remember to enclose a self-addressed, stamped envelope, and be certain to copyright your material first. For more information on copyrighting your material, write to the Registrar of Copyrights, Library of Congress, Washington, DC, 202-707-3000, or go to its Web site at www.loc.gov/copyright. Always put your name and phone number (preferably a service number) on your cards. You never know who will see your work and may want to contact you.

Submission procedures vary among greeting card publishers.

Some prefer individual card ideas on 3-by-5 cards; others prefer receiving a number of complete ideas on 8½-by-11 bond paper. The typical submission includes five to fifteen card ideas with a cover letter.

Income will vary, depending on how much of your work actually sells. Craft shows and flea markets usually charge a booth fee, and you keep all profits. Stores typically pay you half of what each card is sold for. If your work is put into the store on consignment, about 75 percent of the card price is a fair return for you. Greeting card companies and distributors offer individual payment plans, per card payments, and royalties.

You can consult a number of sources for information on the greeting card industry. The book *Writer's Market 2003* contains a listing of greeting card companies and their requirements; the *Greeting Cards Industry Directory* lists names, addresses, and product lines of all exhibitors at the National Stationery Show. Try local bookstores or Amazon.com. Trade magazines, such as *Progressive Greetings* and *Party & Paper Retailer,* may be helpful.

Good luck.

- **BENEFITS:** Working at home; creative outlet; excitement of seeing your work produced.
- **PITFALLS:** Income varies.
- **SOURCES:** Network with craftspeople. Go to card stores, specialty stores, and craft stores. Contact companies listed in *Writer's Market 2003.* Read trade magazines, such as *Progressive Greetings,* 309 Fifth Avenue, New York, NY 10016, www.greetingsmagazine.com; and *Party & Paper Retailer,* www.partypaper.com. For more information, write to Greeting Card Creative Network at 1200 G Street NW, Suite 760, Washington, DC 20005, and the Greeting Card Association, 1350 New York Avenue NW, Suite 615, Washington, DC 20005, 202-393-1778, www.greetingcard.org.

- **NEEDS:** Artistic or photographic talent and vision; marketing ability.
- **IDEAS:** Writing prose for greeting cards is another possibility. If you have the talent, contact card companies with writing samples, using the information above. Check out the book *Sell the Fun Stuff: Writers' and Artists' Market Guidelines for Greeting Cards, Posters, Rubber Stamps, T-Shirts, Aprons, Bumper Stickers, Doormats, and More!* by Jenna Glatzer. Try local bookstores or Amazon.com.

Designing or Refinishing Furniture

Last year I bought a beautiful, distressed wooden coffee table from a soap opera star who started to make and sell furniture after his character had been killed off on his show. What started as a hobby and a way to bring in some extra cash eventually became a lucrative side business. Distressed finishes and colorful, creatively painted furniture are extremely popular right now, and plenty of people and stores alike love to buy custom-made furniture at wholesale prices.

Making or refinishing furniture is fun and creative and challenges your artistic abilities. As a self-employed artist you can create as many or as few pieces as you like or as many as needed to supplement your income. You can sell your own designs or take custom orders, and most important, your schedule is your own.

You need two basic things: a place to work and furniture. The place could be your own backyard, a garage, or a studio. Pieces of furniture are easy to come by and can be gathered from garage sales, flea markets, thrift stores, or even the city dump. I have seen old doorframes turned into desktops and coffee table tops, old school desks stripped and shellacked over with colorful stamps or comic strips, and discarded bathroom furniture pieces painted with vibrant colors and brought back to life. It is exciting to see what one can do with a little imagination and some paint.

The next step of course will be to market the items. Remember, if marketing is not your strength, think about hiring someone to do it for a percentage of the profit. There are a number of ways to sell your furniture: Set up shop right in front of your home on the weekends, and advertise with neighborhood flyers and by word of mouth, or sell your work at flea markets and furniture or craft stores. After you complete a few attractive pieces, have some quality photographs taken, and create a portfolio of your work to show to independent stores. I have seen furniture sellers bring a few of their pieces to flea markets (see "Swap Meets and Flea Markets," this chapter) along with their portfolios and take custom-made orders on the spot. Have business cards handy to pass out to potential customers at these markets.

Another way to sell your work independently (and probably at a higher profit than a store can offer) is by spreading the news among friends. This is exactly how I got my coffee table. The actor who made it traded his work for headshots. I noticed his work at my friend's house and asked for his number. Trade furniture pieces for services or classes, sell discounted pieces to well-connected friends, advertise in local papers, and place flyers on cars. Get your work noticed, and receive a fair price for it.

Your income will depend on how many pieces you sell and your profit margin (including time and material costs). Price similar items at stores, figure out your minimum hourly wage, and negotiate from there.

Good luck.

- **BENEFITS:** Creative outlet; challenging work; self-employment.

- **PITFALLS:** Unsteady salary; time spent gathering wood or furniture.
- **SOURCES:** Flea markets listed in the yellow pages or classifieds under "Swap Meets" and "Flea Markets" or local newspaper weekend calendar sections. Thrift stores. Garage sales. Garbage receptacles.
- **NEEDS:** Artistic talent; patience; tools and paint; wood-working skills.

Factory Go-between

Most people are unaware of many untapped business opportunities. Being a factory go-between is one of them. This is a rep for an established factory or company who sells merchandise for the factory and makes a profit on each item. For example, two law students in New York connected with a factory in the Midwest that manufactures in-line skates and accessories. They negotiated a deal with the factory owners to get merchandise at or below wholesale cost (irregulars and last season's merchandise). They then papered the town and schools with flyers that advertised the names and prices of popular skates and provided a phone number for orders. This concept can be applied to most items (clothing, electronics, and flatware, to name a few) as long as a factory is willing to supply the product.

Working as a factory go-between takes little effort once you get set up and organized. You have no overhead, you spend little time taking orders, and once the factory receives the order, you are out of the picture. The customer pays you, you pay the factory, and the factory sends the merchandise with your logo or label directly to the customer. Make sure you have a clear understanding with the factory that all products must be quality- or size-guaranteed.

Wages are totally dependent on your profit margin (how

much more you charge per item than the factory) and your advertising efforts. Consider selling your item at flea markets (see "Swap Meets and Flea Markets," this chapter).

To hook up with a wholesale distributor or manufacturer, you may need to do some research. Look through various magazines, mail-order ads, newspapers, and the yellow pages for companies selling a product of interest, and then contact the owners, expressing your interest in being a rep.

Good luck.

- **BENEFITS:** Having your own business; little overhead.
- **PITFALLS:** Income varies, depending on product and marketing.
- **SOURCES:** Contacting manufacturers or businesses listed in various magazines. Mail-order ads, newspapers, and the yellow pages.
- **NEEDS:** Marketing ability; product to sell.

Headshot Photographer

There are more than one hundred thousand union actors and probably double that number who are nonunion, and they all need headshots. Not to mention models, musicians, authors, and many others who need publicity prints. The headshot is an actor's calling card. Casting directors need to see a photograph of an actor before he or she is even called in for an audition. In such cities as New York, Los Angeles, Chicago, and Orlando, an inexhaustible supply of actors constantly needs to update their headshots, and busloads of talented transplants migrate each year to entertainment havens, seeking the gold rush of TV and film.

A good headshot photographer must love taking pictures and must have a knack for capturing a person's essence in a photograph (eyes are the key). Being a photographer while pursuing another area in the arts allows you to continue to be creative while earning a living. The job itself includes taking the photographs, developing and reviewing the contact sheets, and selecting the ones you think are best. It's a flexible job in that you are always able to coordinate the time of the shoot with your personal schedule.

If you don't have a background in photography, introductory six- to ten-week photography courses are offered at most community colleges and adult ed schools. The start-up costs for becoming a headshot photographer are reasonable. You will need a decent thirty-five-millimeter camera and lens, which starts at about $275, and, of course, film. Create a portfolio to show prospective clients by shooting volunteer actors and models for free or at cost. Try contacting local agencies for referrals. Shooting a few high-profile clients for free in exchange for a reference will be invaluable in the long run. To promote your business, advertise in the trades and theatrical publications found at performing arts bookstores or newsstands (*Backstage* in several major cities; *Working Actors Guide,* published by Aaron Blake), and post your business cards at theaters and casting offices. Income varies widely: $150 to $2,500 a week, depending on your fee and your bookings. A good photographer charges, on average, $200 to $400 for a two-roll session. This price often includes one or two developed eight-by-tens.

Another way to generate income as a photographer is to take pictures of children at Little League games, karate studios, and other sports and recreational classes. Parents love pictures of their children performing. Or try photographing people at special events. When my husband and I finished the Los Angeles Marathon a number of years ago (have to boast about that!), there was a guy who took our picture and then put it in a plastic circular magnet for a fee. What a great idea! I still have it displayed on my refrigerator. You can also take portraits of people with their pets or their children or even expand to photograph weddings, parties, and other social gatherings. There are endless possibilities to secure employment as a photographer.

Good luck.

- **BENEFITS:** Great profit margin; creative outlet; networking, self-employment; bartering for other services; working at home.
- **PITFALLS:** Unsteady income.
- **SOURCES:** Advertise in theatrical publications found at performing arts bookstores or newsstands: *Backstage* (New York, Los Angeles, Chicago, Miami, Las Vegas), 800-745-8922, www.backstage.com (can be ordered on-line); *Working Actors Guide,* 800-729-6423, www.workingactor.com. Also, place your brochure or cards on bulletin boards at places where actors congregate. Pursue referrals through freebies or agents.
- **NEEDS:** Good thirty-five-millimeter camera and lens; experience; photography course; working well with actors.
- **IDEAS:** *Careers for Shutterbugs and Other Candid Types,* by Cheryl Mclean, offers dozens of career opportunities for anyone who loves working with a camera. Another excellent book is *Photographer's Market: Where and How to Sell Your Photographs,* by Michael Willins. Try local bookstores or Amazon.com.

Home Clothing Sales

Everyone likes a bargain, and home clothing sales provide just that. Home clothing sales involve contacting clothing manufacturers and gathering discounted goods on consignment to sell privately in your home. You will usually receive overcuts (surplus of an item), samples, damaged goods, or last season's merchandise. The manufacturers will tell you what the garments cost, and you can mark them up accordingly to earn a profit.

To run a successful home clothing sale, you will need some specific skills. First, you must be an organized person. It is imperative to keep accurate records of garments sold and how much money each manufacturer is owed. Many manufacturers are willing to give out their clothing only at the end of each season—on consignment, with a promise that you will pick up and return the goods within three days (pick up Friday and return Monday). Another avenue, if you have the cash, is to buy overruns that didn't sell for a variety of reasons or close-out merchandise (irregulars, which are slightly damaged, and discontinued items) below wholesale. This will enable you to sell it all year and then, if desired, you can even take it to a swap meet or flea market (see "Swap Meets and Flea Markets," this chapter). You need space to store garments on racks and a database of customers. Presentation is likewise important. All garments must be steamed, price-tagged, and easily accessible. A mirrored dressing room area, even if it is only a bathroom or bedroom, is essential.

People you know in the clothing industry are great for leads, and often knowing someone in the business is the key to getting merchandise "on loan." Most companies won't trust just anyone with their goods, and you are responsible for all garments taken. If you are looking to buy, check the yellow pages under "Clothing—Wholesale and Manufacturers," and call directly. I suggest asking for a meeting with the production manager, manufacturer, or owner and presenting your idea with authority, conviction, sales ability, and, most important, references!

To let people know about your sale, place flyers where people congregate: yoga centers, salons, supermarkets, health clubs, dance and aerobic studios, and popular audition spots. You may also want to advertise in your community newsletter. Be sure to keep a record of all customers so that you can inform them of the next sale.

Income varies. Some people earn up to $3,000 in a weekend selling clothes. Your success will greatly depend on your merchandise, promotional techniques, and customer base.

Good luck.

- **BENEFITS:** Easy cash; fun; doing it when you want to.
- **PITFALLS:** Unsteady money; need room to store and organize the goods.
- **SOURCES:** Contacts in wholesale manufacturing. Yellow pages under "Clothing—Wholesale and Manufacturers."
- **NEEDS:** Good organization; responsibility; good sales technique; database of customers.

Mail-Order Business

There is a reason that hundreds of companies such as Victoria's Secret send you a "free" catalog every week: It works. Millions of people love the idea of ordering products from the privacy and security of their homes.

This particular moneymaking opportunity is perfect for those with an entrepreneurial spirit. To get started, you need an idea, a PO box to receive orders and payment, and some money for advertising. A few popular ideas are kitschy sexual stuff, gag gifts, information on how to make money fast or get something for free that normally costs money, lists of places to write for free samples, information on how to solve credit problems, recipes, and, of course, the old standbys, diet and beauty products. Money spent on advertising can range from $20 to hundreds of dollars depending on the papers or magazines you choose.

One woman I interviewed ordered by mail a list of foundations that give grants to people looking to consolidate their debts. Upon receiving the information, she was inspired to start her own mail-order business with additional resources she had gathered. She wrote her own flyer, took out an ad in a magazine titled *Jackpot Junkies* (figuring readers would be desperate for her information), and for months after earned substantial money.

To gather ideas, look in magazines and newspapers to see what others are selling. There are a number of books on the subject at your local bookstore or library. A few popular ones are *101 Great Mail-Order Businesses*, by Tyler Hicks, and *How I Made $1,000,000 in Mail Order*, by E. Joseph Cossman.

One final note: To protect a printed product, copyright it. Write to the Registrar of Copyrights, Library of Congress, Washington, DC 20559, 202-707-3000, or visit www.loc.gov/copyright.

Good luck.

- **BENEFITS:** Possibility of making a lot of money easily; working from home; low initial investment if you're selling information.
- **PITFALLS:** Other people see your ad and copy the idea.
- **SOURCES:** Books on the subject to get the business up and running. Magazines and newspapers for ideas.
- **NEEDS:** A good idea; sought-after information or product; money to advertise; ability to write appealing advertisements; perseverance.

Massage Therapist

Massage may be the second-oldest-known profession (the oldest-known profession is not a job this author recommends). It has been practiced for approximately five thousand years. Being a massage therapist has a number of advantages: You are participating in the healing of another person and learning about the human body, which is fascinating. You make a good income with a flexible, part-time schedule once you have established your clientele. You can barter for services like haircuts and privately run classes. Trading massages with other massage therapists is another big plus, not to mention paying off your tuition by giving discounted sessions while attending massage school. Working for a chiropractor, hotel, spa, or gym will pay less than your own service, but it will guarantee you a steady income while you build your client base.

Both the American Massage Therapy Association (AMTA) and the Commission on Massage Therapy Accreditation (COMTA) have comprehensive lists of massage therapy schools in almost every state. You can also check the yellow pages to find massage therapy schools. State requirements differ, so call the local and state board of education or licensing department for information on certification. Also, the AMTA has the requirements of many cities and states posted on its Web site. The National Certification Board for Therapeutic Massage and Bodywork (NCBTMB), a nonprofit organization that is slowly standardizing the industry, offers a national certification exam that requires 500 hours of schooling. Cities and states range in necessary hours of schooling from 150 to 1,000. Many cities have a number of schools that offer eight- to twelve-week part-time courses. For example, the California Healing Arts College offers an eight-week part-time course for $1,895, which is enough for licensing exams in some parts of California. Conversely, the state requirements in New York are rather stringent. You need 1,000 hours of schooling to sit for the New York State licensing exam. The Swedish Institute on West Twenty-sixth Street in New York City offers full-time and part-time options that take, respectively, sixteen months and thirty-two months, for $15,990.

If your finances are tight, there are other options. Many healing arts centers (check your yellow pages or directory assistance) offer massage courses at lower prices. They don't offer certification to practice massage, but they do teach technique and provide information that should enable you to pass the licensing exam in many cities. You can then take other body-related courses at your own pace.

You will also need to buy a massage table, which costs anywhere from $400 to $800 new. For a used table, check your local classifieds or independent papers (the *Recycler* in Los Angeles and the *Village Voice* in New York are excellent) and bulletin boards at massage schools.

Most massage schools have bulletin boards with lists of job openings. Check the help wanted section of the paper for spa and health club job opportunities (see "Working in a Health Club," chapter 4), or contact health clubs directly, using your yellow pages. I know a few people who have bought massage chairs and set up shop in local health markets and office buildings, offering "quickie" massages.

Speak to the manager or owner of a store near you; a short massage in a neighborhood store or, for that matter, in any business could increase sales. Many film producers hire part-time or full-time massage therapists to work on the set, giving relief to the actors.

For a sixty- to ninety-minute massage, the average rate seems to be $65 to $100. Higher rates are common for home visits. For a fifteen-minute neck and shoulder massage, $10 to $18 is the going rate.

Good luck.

- **BENEFITS:** Good wages; meeting different people; contributing to people's health; bartering for services.
- **PITFALLS:** Tuition, building clientele.

- **SOURCES:** American Massage Therapy Association, 847-864-0123, www.amtamassage.org. California Healing Arts College, 310-826-7622, www.chacmassage.com. Swedish Institute, 212-924-5900, www.swedishinstitute.org. Commission on Massage Therapy Accreditation (COMTA), 847-869-5039, ext. 140, www.comta.org. National Certification Board for Therapeutic Massage and Bodywork (NCBTMB), 703-610-9015, automated 1-800-296-0664, www.ncbtmb.com. *Village Voice* (New York), www.villagevoice.com. *Recycler*, www.recycler.com. Classifieds. Yellow pages. Spas and gyms. Chiropractors.
- **NEEDS:** Education; certification; massage license.

Mobile Auto Detailing

Mobile auto detailing is a popular service, especially in cities with frequent inclement weather or air pollution. People are always willing to pay good money to keep their cars in top shape. Mobile auto detailing involves driving to your client's car and giving it a thorough cleaning inside and out, shampooing the seats and carpeting, and polishing and buffing all interior and exterior surfaces.

Going into business for yourself, or with a partner, as an auto detailer can be quite lucrative. Owning your own business guarantees flexibility. Like many of the jobs in this book, auto detailing can also be used to barter for other services. An actor I know who does mobile auto detailing trades his services for headshots and classes. Keep in mind that you must be in decent physical condition, as this job involves physical labor.

To gain the necessary knowledge and experience, work for an auto detailing shop first (check the yellow pages), or get your own car detailed by a mobile unit and ask specific business questions. To start your own auto detailing business, you will have to invest approximately $1,500 to $2,500, which will cover the cost of all the equipment you will need. To make things easier, you may want to have built a trailer that hooks up to the back of your car and enables you to carry the necessities, like a gasoline power pump, generator, steamer, and polisher. Most important, you must obtain a license. For information on obtaining a license or certificate, call your city's tax and permit division or the county clerk's office. It is also a good idea to check with your car insurance agent for quotes on minor insurance since you will be dealing with other people's personal property.

Naturally, to build a good customer base, you will need to advertise your services. Word of mouth is always the best way to generate interest, but flyers are also quite effective. Public garages and professional office complexes are great places to target steady customers: They can afford regular service, and you can polish their cars during their business hours. Ideally, you should find steady clients who will employ your services on a monthly basis. Another idea is to hire yourself out to auto dealers, who often like to "prep" cars for sale.

The process of mobile auto detailing a car typically takes two to three hours. The going rate is $150 to $300 for the job. As in most jobs, the harder you work, the more money you will make.

Good luck.

- **BENEFITS:** Lucrative work; flexible hours.
- **PITFALLS:** Hard physical labor; start-up costs; securing customers.
- **SOURCES:** Yellow pages. Work at an auto shop for experience. Advertise in local papers, distribute flyers at professional office complexes. Check out MobileWorks at www.mobileworks.com and Detail King at www.detail king.com or 800-939-6601.

- **NEEDS:** A car; insurance; money for equipment; experience; sales technique.

Mobile Disc Jockey

These days most people are on budgets, and the cost of a band or full orchestra for an event can really put a dent in the wallet. A DJ is more cost-effective than hiring a full band, and many people actually prefer DJs, so they get to hear their favorite songs sung by the original artists. There is nothing worse than a guy in a cheap tuxedo doing his version of a Bruce Springsteen classic. A DJ's duties include MCing, spinning records, and getting people on the dance floor. Playing appropriate music during the event is essential—for example, classical during mealtime and swing and top forty for dancing. This is a great job for musicians or anyone who loves music, people, and parties. The ideal DJ possesses an extensive knowledge of current music as well as popular oldies. Above all, he or she must have the ability to feel out the crowd and know intuitively what music they want to hear. I was warned by a number of DJs that some parties, especially children's parties, can be high-maintenance, since parents tend to transfer a lot of their anxiety on to you. According to my sources, corporate and college parties are less stressful.

If you are just starting out, I suggest that you intern with another DJ to learn the ropes. You can earn $100-plus a night changing CDs or records while the DJ uses the microphone and plays games. To work for an established entertainment company, check the yellow pages under "Disc Jockeys" and "Entertainers."

When the time comes to start your own business, you will need to buy or rent equipment: a few good speakers, an amp, a mixer, and a turntable (the old-fashioned way) or a special two-CD player with pitch control. This equipment can be purchased at most specialty music stores and will cost approximately $3,000. You will also need about a hundred CDs. Join a few of the music clubs advertised in newspapers and magazines, such as Columbia House and BMG; you can get a lot of free and discounted music. Putting together a demo tape for review by prospective parties is essential to your success. To generate business, you can work some free or discounted gigs—church, temple, college, or theater company parties would be good places to start—and pass out your business cards. Advertise in your local paper or on bulletin boards. As always, word of mouth is the best advertisement.

The standard rate for a DJ is typically $125 to $300 an hour. If you are a novice, I suggest a rate of about $100 an hour until you develop a reputation. There is usually a four-hour minimum. You can always charge time and a half if the host wants you to play beyond the previously scheduled hours.

Most of the DJs I spoke to emphasized the importance of being on time, presentable (a suit for most parties), and accommodating. One DJ said he is always set up and ready to go thirty to sixty minutes before the event begins. Remember, the host is counting on you for the success of the party.

Good luck.

- **BENEFITS:** Fun; meeting people; learning music; good pay.
- **PITFALLS:** Unsteady cash flow if it's your own business.
- **SOURCES:** Yellow pages under "Disc Jockey" and "Entertainers."
- **NEEDS:** Professional behavior; knowledgeability in current music and oldies; equipment and CDs if it's your own business; advertising.

Music Teacher

Music teachers are always needed, for there are always children (and adults!) excited to learn how to play instruments. Many people try several instruments before they decide on one, and therefore introductory classes are common. You don't need a master's degree to teach a beginner's class at an adult education center and at some music institutions. Piano and guitar are particularly popular instruments to learn, but any instrument, including voice, can also be taught privately.

If you don't want to work at an established music center, you will need to advertise to find students. Most music instructors who start teaching on their own begin with private lessons. Promote yourself by posting flyers at music stores and universities, contacting music teachers at schools, and via classifieds. The Internet is a good vehicle for self-promotion, especially through on-line classifieds. Craigslist is a popular site and has classifieds for many major cities in the United States. You can also register with various groups that will place you on a list that is available to students looking for a teacher. You don't need any formal education to register with the Music Teachers List at www.teach list.com, and it is free as well. If you want to go a step further, the Music Teachers National Association is one of the oldest and largest nonprofit music teachers' associations. It offers a certification exam that will allow you to be on its list of accredited teachers.

For private lessons, most people charge anywhere from $25 to $60 per session. Sessions are usually either half an hour or an hour. If you are just starting out, you'll want to charge at the low end of the spectrum. I know a drummer who is just starting to teach, and he's offering a one-hour lesson for $20. What you charge also depends on the length of the session, your experience and education, and travel time. Some music instructors travel to clients' homes, while others have the clients come to them. It depends on the instrument and on the client's circumstances. Clearly, if you are traveling to your client's home, it is reasonable to charge a bit more.

As in most professions, it can be much more profitable to work privately. However, if stable income is important to you, and you dislike self-promotion, working at a music center or school is the more logical choice. Check the yellow pages under "Music Instruction" for local music centers and schools.

Good luck.

- **BENEFITS:** Flexible schedule; self-employment; low initial investment; creative opportunities.
- **PITFALLS:** Gathering students; teaching what you would rather be doing.
- **SOURCES:** Call institutions about teaching requirements. Check yellow pages under "Music Instruction." Craigslist, www.craigslist.org.; Music Teachers List, www.teachlist. com. Music Teachers National Association, 888-512-5278, www.mtna.org.
- **NEEDS:** Love of music; an instrument if you plan to teach out of your home; patience; good communication skills.

Multilevel Marketing

Multilevel marketing (MLM) has been hailed by many as an amazing way to earn money. Almost anyone can be successful at it with a little work, planning, and a belief in the product or service being sold. The whole idea of multilevel or network marketing is to sell a product or service directly to others, who then become users and potential new sellers (your downline). You (the original seller) get a commission on both your individual sales and your downline sales. The more people who sell for you in your downline, the more money you make. For example, selling to five customers each of whom sells to five others creates twenty-five customers from whom you receive commissions. Depending on the number of people in your downline, untold numbers of customers are possible.

A major plus of this job is being able to work from your home. You create your own work schedule. On the downside, though, since this is a commission only job, income fluctuates. Additionally, you may need to spend money to familiarize yourself with the products you will be selling. A few popular MLM companies you may have heard of include Herbalife, Nu Skin, and Melaleuca.

MLM typically involves signing an agreement with the provider of a product or service to become a personal user and to market to others. With some companies there is a sign-up fee. Also, a minimum commitment to stock inventory is often required or advisable so you have samples or demonstrators for prospective customers. Be careful not to become involved with an MLM company that requires you to buy and stock more products than can be easily used or sold. The marketing plans of MLM companies vary considerably, as do the terms and conditions of the contracts. The most lucrative usually involve consumable products that customers use and reorder, like cosmetics, cleaners, vitamins, or long-distance phone carriers. Consumable products produce residual income, a monthly profit generated after the initial sale on the basis of reorders. Income varies considerably, depending on the product and your marketing abilities. Some people make as much as $40,000 a month, and others make a few hundred a month.

There are thousands of MLM companies to choose from. Visit www.onlinemlm.com for a comprehensive list of them. Any reputable MLM company will provide frequent informational seminars.

Good luck.

- **BENEFITS:** Self-employment; opportunity for high income and residuals; flexible hours; working out of home.
- **PITFALLS:** Commission only; spending money to familiarize yourself with the product; sometimes stocking high-volume inventory.
- **SOURCES:** Online MLM at www.onlinemlm.com.
- **NEEDS:** Belief in product/service; entrepreneurial spirit.

Party Promoter

Were you the kid who invited two hundred friends over to your house as soon as your parents went out of town? Have you ever been at a party, specifically a singles event, and thought, "I could plan a much more interesting party than this!" Well, here is a job for you.

College students, young professionals, people in their forties on up, Christian and Jewish singles, and vegetarians are attracted to great parties as a way to meet other like-minded individuals. Party promoters put these parties together. Judging from the city and climate you live in, you'll need to find an interesting venue to hold a party in and an eye-catching way to promote it. Depending on the age you're catering to, sports parties, ballroom or swing dancing parties, or virtual reality parties can be much more interesting and successful than the usual affair with a rented room and a DJ.

One party promoter told me he always keeps track of new places by reading various publications and local magazines that review "hot spots." Recently he read an article on a new café that opened as part of a boathouse. He rented it for a night and had a successful party called Party on the Dock of the Bay.

Successful parties require promotion, direct mailing, and advertising. Word of mouth is always best. Send out simple postcards to keep costs minimal, or create elaborate invitations in hopes of attracting a larger, more exclusive crowd. When your parties are a hit, your mailing list will grow and people will return to the events you organize.

When going into business, contact your local county clerk's office to set up a corporation, self-proprietorship, or partnership. Liability insurance is important as well. When booking a space, you can go in person or handle arrangements by phone. You may need to give a deposit and show a portfolio with past invitations and write-ups. Salary will vary, depending on how successful your party is when compared with costs involved. When you book a place, you typically guarantee a certain number of people or bar revenue. Earnings can vary from a few hundred bucks a party up to $10,000.

Good luck.

- **BENEFITS:** Flexible hours; social connections; potential to earn a lot of money.
- **PITFALLS:** Promotion costs; stress at time of parties; feeling responsible for people having a good time.
- **SOURCES:** When starting a business, perhaps team up with such organizations as temples, churches, and dating services; finding venues to hold parties.
- **NEEDS:** Business acumen; liability insurance; promotional talents.

Personal Shopper

Are you always on the best-dressed list? If you have an eye for color and the ability to make wise fashion decisions and you enjoy shopping, consider becoming a personal shopper. Personal shoppers give personal assistance to customers according to their needs and tastes. By hiring you, clients will actually save money by making specific purchases that satisfy their needs.

You also help clients weed out unworn, unflattering, or outdated items in their wardrobes.

Department stores hire personal shoppers, or you can choose to work independently. Department stores often look for personal shoppers who have retail experience and a design background or a flair for fashion. Working for a department store will enable you to know when all the sales are to assist your customer and give you a steady paycheck; department stores usually give commissions plus salaries. On the downside, you are limited to choosing clothes from that particular store, and because you are working on commission, you may feel pressure to "sell" the client, which may not be in his or her best interest. Working independently allows for greater freedom, albeit an irregular paycheck. Your job often consists of going through your client's closet and deciding what works and what doesn't: spring cleaning! If you work independently, it is valuable to have an in with wholesale houses.

Pay varies. You can earn anywhere from $25,000 to $100,000 annually as a personal shopper. Some personal shoppers gather percentage fees of what is actually purchased, and in that case it depends on your clients and the items they're buying. In general, the more expensive the items, the more money you earn. At showrooms the client saves money on the items purchased, and the shopper can often receive up to 20 percent of the actual sale.

For employment in a department store, contact human resources, or look in the classifieds. Independent work is often obtained by word of mouth. Advertise in local papers and in community, church, or temple newsletters. Place ads at salons and health clubs. Offer to barter your services when starting out to spread the word.

Good luck.

- **BENEFITS:** Flexible hours; fun to shop; assisting clients.
- **PITFALLS:** In department stores, you're limited to their

clothing. When you're self-employed, work can be unsteady, and it may take time to gather a clientele.

- **SOURCES:** Department stores. Advertising. Word of mouth. Yellow pages and the Internet under "Shopping Service."
- **NEEDS:** Fashion and color sense; people skills; knowledge of various manufacturers.
- **IDEAS:** Being an image consultant is a rewarding and lucrative field as well.

Personal Organizer

Is your motto "A place for everything and everything in its place"? Can you find whatever you need at a moment's notice because your home and office are so well organized? Have you honed the fine art of a clutter-free lifestyle? If you answered yes to these questions, being a personal organizer may be a terrific job for you.

Personal organizers help their clients—both businesses and individuals—get their offices or homes in order by setting up filing systems to help manage paperwork, organizing overflowing closets, and reconfiguring work areas for optimal use of space. This involves helping clients weed out unused objects, papers, clothes, and other items that are taking up space and creating confusion. Often people need help (and encouragement) in deciding what to throw away. Once you've helped them get rid of their clutter, you can work with clients to install such items as storage bins, shelves, and drawers to help organize the things that survived the clutter cut. You will need to be able to organize in a logical and useful way by putting frequently used items in easily accessible places and creating an order that both makes sense to the client and is consistent with his or her lifestyle. One personal organizer I spoke with told me that one of her clients used to keep her umbrellas in her bedroom closet. No wonder she could never find one when she needed it!

You will need very good interpersonal skills and the ability to be flexible. Remember, you will be stepping into somone's personal, sometimes very private space, so you need to be able to respect others' tastes and wishes and present your proposed changes in a thoughtful, tactful manner. By hiring you, clients will save time and create more space in their lives. A well-organized room, office, and home can bring sanity to even the most chaotic of lifestyles.

Both individuals and businesses hire personal organizers. You may choose to work independently or for an established company. Check in the yellow pages under "Organizing Services—Household & Business." Pay varies. It is customary to charge businesses more than individuals. As an independent personal organizer, expect to earn $40 to $100 per hour. Although businesses will pay on the higher end, they will also want more experience. Many personal organizers have a minimum amount of hours that you have to hire them for. This sometimes depends on travel time. One organizer I interviewed has a two-hour minimum for people within her immediate area and three hours for those farther away. Another one I spoke with had a three-hour minimum for everyone. Independent work is often obtained by word of mouth. On-line classifieds such as Craigslist, local papers, and community newsletters are good places to advertise. In addition, you could put flyers and business cards on bulletin boards at churches, temples, and other community centers. Place ads at salons and health clubs, or offer to barter your services when starting out to spread the word. There is a National Association of Professional Organizers in Norcoss, Georgia, with fourteen chapters across the country.

Good luck!

- **BENEFITS:** Flexible schedule; helping people.
- **PITFALLS:** When you are self-employed, work can be unsteady, and it may take time to gather a clientele.
- **SOURCES:** National Association of Professional Organizers, 770-325-3440, www.napo.net. Professional Organizers Web Ring, www.organizerswebring.com. On-line classifieds such as Craigslist, www.craigslist.org. Advertising. Word of mouth. Yellow pages under "Organizing Services—Household & Business."
- **NEEDS:** Excellent organizational skills; people skills; knowledge of various methods for organizing clothes, papers, and other things.

Personal Chef

Do you love cooking but hate the mundane chopping and assembly-line cooking you end up doing if you're not the head chef at a restaurant? Being someone's personal chef will allow you to be king of the kitchen and make money doing what you love. People who don't have time to cook or have conditions preventing them from preparing meals themselves hire personal chefs to come to their homes and "batch cook." This is an especially popular service with working parents who want to feed their children home-cooked meals but don't have the time or energy (or skill) to do it.

Personal chefs can be hired once a week, twice a week, once every two weeks, or just on special occasions. It really depends on the needs of the client. Some people want someone to come once every two weeks and prepare foods that can be frozen and used as desired. A personal chef I know worked for two families twice a week each, and that was all the work she needed to make a good living. Another personal chef I know gave her client lessons as she cooked for her. Some people will prefer to purchase the food themselves and will want you to cook at their house. Others want you to keep the mess in your own home and will reimburse you for the groceries.

Many personal chefs work for people who have special diets. Some people who look for this service want to lose weight or are suffering from food allergies, diabetes, cancer, or heart disease. This last kind of specialized cooking often pays more. It might be necessary to do some research on the particular condition to find suitable dishes to prepare. You may also be asked to find ways of preparing traditional dishes with alternative ingredients—for example, baking a birthday cake for a diabetic or for someone with a wheat allergy.

Special training will not be necessary if you have a lot of experience cooking, although you may want to take several classes at your local culinary institute to fill in any gaps in your knowledge. Another option is to enroll in a chef-training program. If you decide to pursue such a program, it might be prudent to attend one of the natural-cooking schools, which tend to focus on the healing benefits of food and cooking for people with common ailments. Three schools with such a focus are the Natural Gourmet Cookery School in New York City, the Institute for Educational Therapy (IET) in Cotati, California, and the Natural Epicurean Academy of Culinary Arts in Austin, Texas. A full training program consists of about 400 to 600 hours of schooling an will cost you anywhere from $5,000 to $15,000. For $14,850, the Natural Gourmet Cookery School in Manhattan offers a 616-hour chef-training program, which you can do either full-time or part-time. The IET is 405 hours and is one of the most affordable choices at $5,600. Both the IET and Natural Gourmet Cookery are state-licensed, and Natural Gourmet Cookery offers individual classes for about $75 to $200. For a list of cooking schools, check out *The Guide to Cooking Schools 2003*, published by ShawGuides. Also, CulinaryEd.com and

CulinaryInstitutes.com have nationwide lists of schools. Remember, this job is something you can do without specialized training; however, if you don't have cooking school or work experience under your belt, you will need to prove yourself.

You will want to create business cards and either a menu or a brochure with a list of foods you can prepare and a little bit about your specialty (if you have one). Some specialties are Chinese cooking, vegetarian cooking, and diabetic cooking. An economical way to make professional-looking business cards and brochures or menus is to design them yourself and have them printed by a printing and copy center like Kinko's. Any computer superstore will have several inexpensive, easy-to-use programs that are specifically for creating brochures. Also, a word processing program like Microsoft Word can be used to create both your business cards and your brochure or menu. If you don't feel comfortable doing it yourself, you could hire a graphic arts student from a local college for a small fee or trade your cooking talents for a friend's computer skills.

Marketing yourself is the next step. You will need to post your business cards, brochures or menus, and flyers on community bulletin boards. Health food and natural health stores, gyms, and beauty stores are great places to start. Day care centers that have bulletin boards are also good, and you may want to give some flyers or brochures to friends and family members who work at large companies. Many offices have community boards that accept such flyers. If you are even slightly computer-savvy, you can build yourself a Web site. Tripod, Angelfire, and GeoCities give free sites that offer plenty of space so you can include graphics. Again, you could have a graphic arts student create the Web site for you, or you could barter your services to get this done. Once you have the site created, it is important that you register it with search engines like Google and Yahoo. To register with Google, go to www.google.com/addurl.html, and for Yahoo, to docs. yahoo.com/info/suggest/. Word of mouth is still probably one of the best ways to become popular, but you may also want to put a classified ad in your local paper if it's not too pricey.

You can charge anywhere from $15 to $50 per hour, depending on your experience and training. If you have no formal training and no experience, you might want to start at $15. If you have education but no experience, $25 is a reasonable charge, and if you have schooling and experience cooking in a restaurant, but it's your first time being a personal chef, you can ask for $35.

If self-promotion is your weak point, you may want to consider working for a company that will find clients for you. Big City Chefs, 866-321-CHEF, is one of several national companies that provide corporations and individuals with personal chefs. This agency has offices in Los Angeles, San Francisco, Chicago, Washington, D.C., New York City, and elsewhere, but it requires either a culinary degree or three years of professional culinary experience.

Good luck.

- **BENEFITS:** Contributing to people's health; self-employment; creative outlet; bartering for services.
- **PITFALLS:** Securing customers or building clientele; unsteady income.
- **SOURCES:** New York: Natural Gourmet Cookery School, 212-645-5170, www.naturalgourmetschool.com. Chicago: Cooking and Hospitality Institute of Chicago, www. houseofedu.com/chic/. Los Angeles: California School of Culinary Arts, www.houseofedu.com/csca/. California: Institute for Educational Therapy, Cotati campus: 800-987-7530; Santa Cruz campus: 831-457-1207; www. iet.org. Washington, D.C.: Friends & Food International,

Inc., 202-726-4616. Austin: Natural Epicurean Academy of Culinary Arts, 512-476-2276, www.naturalepicurean. com. National information: American Personal Chef Association, 800-644-8389, www.personalchef.com; United States Personal Chef Association, 800-995-2138, www.uspca.com; CulinaryEd.com, www.culinaryed.com; CulinaryInstitutes.com, www.culinary-institutes.com.Shaw Guides, 212-799-6464, http://cookingcareer.shawguides. com/. Big City Chefs, 866-321-CHEF. To build a Web site, check out: www.tripod.lycos.com; www.angelfire. lycos.com; www.geocities.yahoo.com.

- **NEEDS:** Love of cooking; training or experience; some self-promotion ability.

Plant Leasing and Maintenance

Given the concrete jungles we live in today, having greenery around us has become both a necessity and a trend. A restaurant may have as many as forty to fifty plants, banks with the typical high ceilings may have twelve to fifteen very large plants, and hotel lobbies are filled with greenery. A plant leasing and maintenance business involves leasing and caring for these plants and assuring customers of weekly visits to keep the plants healthy and attractive.

You will need to have a general knowledge of familiar plants since each type has different light, water, and food requirements. Some of the specifics you will have to learn are: Which plants can thrive behind tinted windows? What is the impact of direct and indirect sunlight? Which plants are low in pollen? Which plants are the heartiest? Reading books and working in a plant store or greenhouse are good ways to learn about these basic characteristics.

Many existing services supply rental and maintenance agreements. To work for an existing business (a great way to learn the ropes), look in the yellow pages under "Plants, Interior Design and Maintenance" and "Live Plant Rental & Leasing." To start your own business, try to work out an agreement with a neighborhood nursery for discounts on supplies and plants. A large vehicle is necessary for transportation of plants; use your own or rent a truck as needed. Some nurseries may even be willing to transport and care for the plants if you act as the leasing agent.

You will need to advertise your services in local papers and by word of mouth. Or you can create a flyer and distribute it to your target markets. Income will vary, depending on the number of steady clients you have. To find out competitive pricing, call a few companies listed in the yellow pages. The average monthly rent is 15 to 20 percent of the wholesale price. Leasing a few plants to an office will probably cost it a minimum of $100 per month. Leasing a plant such as a ficus for an empty home up for sale (so it looks more attractive to potential buyers) costs about $20 per week.

Good luck.

- **BENEFITS:** Self-employment; great for plant lovers.
- **PITFALLS:** Unsteady income until regular clientele is established.
- **SOURCES:** Yellow pages under "Plants, Interior Design and Maintenance." Visiting local nurseries and working out a deal.
- **NEEDS:** Plant knowledge; green thumb; marketing abilities.
- **IDEAS:** A similar approach can be applied to aquarium maintenance for all you fish lovers out there!

Product Manufacturer "Artisan"

Was arts and crafts always one of your favorite classes as a kid? Who would have guessed that your artistic talents might actually have a practical use and allow you to generate a more than substantial income? There is a wealth of success stories in this field, from the young women who invented "hard candy" nail polishes to your neighbor designing and selling jewelry. I have interviewed many people who use their creative skills on a small scale by selling to specialty stores, as well as those who have eventually expanded to hire reps all over the world and become the owners of million-dollar corporations.

A few ideas that have worked in the past are dipped plaster pieces (the angel craze), custom-made pillows and tapestries, gift baskets, hats, candles, uniquely designed lampshades, mirrors and frames, dress designing, bath oils, and flavored cooking oils in decorative bottles. Craft magazines sold at newsstands will also fuel you with ideas.

There are many ways to market your product. You can do it personally by bartering your crafts or giving them as gifts; that will spread the word and create other inquiries and sales. A woman recently thanked me for a simple suggestion that I gave her at a seminar of mine. She wanted to get her cake-decorating business off the ground, so I told her to get business cards made up and to start volunteering to bake the cake for celebratory functions and private parties as her gift. Word traveled quickly, and soon she was the owner of a successful cake-decorating business.

You can sell your products and network at flea markets and fairs (see "Swap Meets and Flea Markets," this chapter). Find out where art shows are taking place and where the main mart in your city is located. Marts often have reps to meet with. Reps require commissions—10 percent for clothing lines and 15 to

20 percent for accessories are standard—but they can really broaden the market for your product. If you have good marketing skills, you may want to approach local dealers and shop owners. You can also sell your stuff through the Internet. The Craft Site Directory is a good resource for this. I know people who have set up entire businesses taking orders via the Internet, shipping packages right from their homes.

Earning potential varies greatly, from a few thousand dollars a year to millions, depending on how much energy you invest in your business. On the plus side, this type of work can often be started with minimal initial investment. And as orders come in, so will deposits to offset costs.

Good luck.

- **BENEFITS:** Creative outlet; working at home, flexible schedule; being your own boss; adding beauty to the world.
- **PITFALLS:** Often slow process of making, selling, and marketing the products.
- **SOURCES:** Craft Site Directory, www.craftsitedirectory.com.
- **NEEDS:** Creativity; imagination; ability to put colors and textures together; artistic skills.

Résumé Service

In today's ultracompetitive market, everyone needs a professional résumé. It's a person's calling card, it makes a statement, and it sets the candidate apart from hundreds of others. Not everyone has the time, the inclination, or the know-how to create a top-notch résumé, and that's where a résumé service comes in.

A résumé service can provide any of the following: advice on résumé content and style, format design, computer storage of the résumé for updates, and laser copies of the résumé. Some services also do bios, cover letters, logos, labels, and personalized mailers. You can set up your résumé service to deal with a specific group or profession or broaden it to deal with the general public's needs—whatever most suits you. A friend of mine started the very popular résumé service for actors called Imagestarter, based in Los Angeles. His theatrical photo résumés combine an actor's headshot on the same page as his or her credits.

Flexibility is a major advantage here since you can set your own hours and work out of your home. To run a résumé service, you need a computer, disks, a word processing program, and a laser printer. Computer proficiency and a thorough understanding of résumé writing, formats, and content are building blocks of your success. It is also important to be able to offer different aesthetically pleasing designs. Libraries usually have several different résumé books, or you can purchase one from a bookstore. If you have a high-quality laser printer and a few quality paper choices, you can charge money to make copies too.

To get started, advertise in local publications and trade papers. If you are marketing to a specific profession, such as medical doctors, advertise at hospitals, clinics, and the trade papers found at medical school bookstores and newsstands. Of course word of mouth is best.

Find out the going rate for designing a résumé by calling competitors in your area. Designing a work résumé for the general public usually costs $100 to $250. Updates typically are about $25 to $50. It takes approximately an hour to design a résumé. Certain cases may require a consulting fee.

Good luck.

- **BENEFITS:** Working out of your home; being your own boss.
- **PITFALLS:** Unsteady income.

- **SOURCES:** Advertise in local publications or in populated places. Word of mouth.
- **NEEDS:** Computer; printer; programs.

Secretarial/Word Processing Service

There's an important reason for National Secretaries Day: No office or business can run efficiently without a top-quality secretary or assistant. These days freelance secretaries are in demand because many companies are scaling back and sizing down, preferring to contract out for individual projects. Large corporations and hospitals have enormous monthly dictation and transcription needs, not to mention the small business owners or individuals who need occasional assistance.

Secretarial and administrative services can involve organizing offices and files, answering phones, setting appointments, typing manuscripts, sending out mass mailings, doing personal and business correspondence, and performing special job-specific tasks. Some services also include desktop publishing, graphic design services, and personalized mailers.

For employment with an established company, you can work through a temp agency (see "Temp Work," chapter 6) listed in the yellow pages, or look through the classified section of your paper under "Secretary" and "Administrative Assistant." Working through a temp agency allows you to learn the ropes before starting your own business.

To begin your own service, you will need such business supplies as a computer, a printer, a fax machine, business cards, stationery supplies, and a word processing program. I recommend you read a few books on starting a home business as well as on freelance secretarial services. It is also helpful to keep handy books on proper grammar, punctuation, and business-style writing. It may take more time and energy to start your own business, but in the end the monetary rewards will be greater than working for someone else. Additionally, you are eligible for tax deductions when working out of your home, and your hours can be as flexible as you desire.

Advertising your services in the yellow pages or trade publications, such as *Backstage*, a publication for performing artists, and *Publishers Weekly*, are good ways to get the word out. Go to a newsstand, flip through some papers and magazines, and decide which ones might prove lucrative to advertise in. The pay will vary from project to project. You have to set a fair hourly wage for your time and expertise and price your services accordingly. An easy way to do this is to call other secretarial services to determine the fair market value. Profits will depend on location, efficiency, and hustle. You can even include a pickup and delivery charge for your services.

Good luck.

- **BENEFITS:** Flexible hours; working out of your home.
- **PITFALLS:** Up-front costs to purchase supplies and equipment.
- **SOURCES:** Temp agencies. Advertising in local publications and at populated places. *Backstage*, 800-745-8922, www.backstage.com; *Publishers Weekly*, 866-456-0410, www.publishersweekly.com.
- **NEEDS:** Excellent knowledge of computers and secretarial skills.

Sketch Artist

This is a fun, creative job for someone who has sketch portrait skills or a fashion illustrator/designer background. You can find work as a sketch artist in a variety of industries. Storyboards (sketches of each scene in a script) are used to help directors visualize different scenes for TV and film projects. Comic book publishers often need to seek out artists. Sketching portraits or caricatures at parties (especially popular at bar and bat mitzvahs) and social functions is also a possibility. Another interesting job for someone who draws well is as a police identification artist at a sheriff's office, although this is more appropriate for someone who is experienced at sketching from a verbal description.

If you are just beginning, you may want to offer your services for free so you can put together a portfolio and make contacts. Student films and nonunion commercials can be a great place to start. Check the trades for advertisements—for example, *Sketch Magazine,* which is a trade publication for comics. When you have accumulated enough sketches, create a portfolio of your best work that demonstrates the breadth of your skills. Ascertain the proper contact persons at a variety of studios, and set up appointments to show your portfolio. If you can't get an appointment, you may be able to drop off your work. Then your potential employers can review it on their own time. As always, use any contacts you have. The *Pacific Coast Studio Directory* (the yellow pages of studios in Los Angeles), the *New York Production Guide* (NYPG), the *Illinois Production Guide, LA 411*, and the *Hollywood Creative Directory* are a few books that can assist you in finding studios and production companies. They as well as others are available at performing arts bookstores or may be ordered by mail from Samuel French Theater & Film Bookstore, 7623 Sunset Boulevard, Los Angeles, CA 90046, 800-8ACT-NOW, www.samuelfrench.com. Samuel French, Inc. has stores not only in California but in New York, Canada, and England.

To advertise your service for parties, contact party planners by looking in the yellow pages under "Party Planning Services" and "Entertainers." You can also advertise in the classified sections of local papers and magazines. A parents' magazine can be a terrific resource.

For storyboard artists, pay will vary, depending on union versus nonunion work. Salary is negotiable for independent jobs depending on how much work is actually needed. When negotiating, decide what is equitable for your time and talent on a daily or hourly basis. Call some competitors in your area to find out the going rate.

Good luck.

- **BENEFITS:** Creative and fun work; networking opportunities.
- **PITFALLS:** Irregular work; variable wages; tough to get started.
- **SOURCES:** For storyboard work, the *Pacific Coast Studio Directory*, the *New York Production Guide* (NYPG), the *Hollywood Creative Directory*, the *Illinois Production Guide*, and *LA 411*. Industry contacts. *Sketch Magazine*, 859-282-0096, www.bluelinepro.com/sketch.htm. Samuel French Theater & Film Bookstore, 800-8ACT-NOW, www.samuel french.com.
- **NEEDS:** Sketching and portraiture skills.

Start Your Own 900 Number

The 900 number industry started in 1984. MCI, Sprint, and AT&T entered the field in 1987, and by 1989 certain financial and administrative changes allowed entrepreneurs and small businesses to get involved. Since 1991 the 900 number industry has made about $1 billion in revenue per year, translating into vast and varied opportunities for budding entrepreneurs.

Because of new FCC regulations, the 900 number image is more acceptable now (it used to be associated strictly with phone sex lines). It has been reshaped by the interest of Fortune 500 companies. *Consumer Reports*, the *Wall Street Journal*, the Better Business Bureau, Procter & Gamble, and the pope all have used 900 numbers. Examples of 900 services include opinion polls, stock information, jokes, customer or product support, and horoscopes. Hundreds of professionals and celebrities are providing information while making money.

Not surprisingly, a 900 number can be extremely profitable for you as well. Basically, a 900 service is a caller-paid service that provides access to a variety of information and entertainment. You simply get an idea and put it on a 900 number, and the long-distance carrier does the billing and collecting. Costs vary greatly, depending on what you set up with the service bureau and your advertising budget. Expect to spend a few hundred dollars on the low end to a few thousand dollars and up on the high end. If you work through a service bureau, your initial costs can be on the low end because the service bureau buys the hardware and software, hires the programmer, sets up the line, gets it approved by the long-distance carrier, and provides necessary support. If you want to be really hands off about it, you can get the bureau to answer prerecorded calls for you. In return, the service bureau gets a percentage of your business. The 900 service bureau subscribes directly to a common carrier, such as MCI, by leasing multiple 900 numbers directly. Call your long-distance company for further information. For $4, MCI will give you information on the 900 service, including guidelines, and a list of service bureaus. Do your research and choose the service bureau that meets your needs from the many available. In addition, many independent adult learning schools such as the Learning Annex (found in a number of major cities) have offered courses on starting a 900 number company. Another idea is to visit a library in your area, locate books and articles on the subject, and research your options. A popular book on the subject is *900 Know-How: How to Succeed with Your Own 900 Number Business,* by Robert Mastin and Carol Morse Ginsburg.

Initially, you will need cash flow to market your line, but since a lot of money can be made with these numbers, you may recoup quickly. A number of years ago a physician in Los Angeles started a 900 number line called Be Abused While Being Amused, offering a different insulting joke each day. At one point he was making thousands of dollars a day! Cleverness and timing can pay off. But be warned, this kind of income is the exception, not the rule.

A neighbor of mine, experienced in the 900 number industry, but not as lucky as the physician mentioned above, advises anyone serious about making money in today's marketplace to devise a service line that provides hard, fact-based information that is difficult or impossible to obtain elsewhere. He suggests hooking up with a professional, such as a doctor, lawyer, or real estate broker, and giving prerecorded, factual information for which there is an established need.

When it comes to marketing, consider hiring an ad agency to help develop a campaign. It is money well spent because the ad is all you have to present to make the initial connection with your audience. Another idea is to get a media partner so you don't have to pay for ads. I think a successive strategy would be to hook up with a tabloid television program, using the 900 number as a poll to interact with the show's audience.

Good luck.

- **BENEFITS:** Chance to make a huge profit; hands-off business if prerecorded.
- **PITFALLS:** Up-front costs; advertising expenses; irregular income.
- **SOURCES:** MCI, 900-733-6249. The Learning Annex for a course: San Francisco, 415-788-5500; San Diego, 619-544-9700; Los Angeles, 310-478-6677; New York, 212-371-0280; and Toronto, 416-964-0011, www.learningannex.

com. The library for books and magazine articles: *The Directory of 900 Service Bureaus: How to Select One,* by Audiotex News; *900 Know-How: How to Succeed with Your Own 900 Number Business,* by Robert Mastin and Carol Morse Ginsburg, 401-849-4200. Service bureaus include; JCN, 561-272-5667, www.jcnltd.com; Network Telephone Services, 800-727-6874; MMI/America's Best 900#, 800-664-9007, www.best900.com; and Scherers Communications, 800-555-3090, www.scherers.com.

- **NEEDS:** An idea; a 900 number.

Swap Meets and Flea Markets

The concept of swap meets took off in California in the early sixties, and today thousands of them are held regularly across the nation. One of the largest flea markets in the country is the monthly Rose Bowl Swap Meet in Pasadena, held on the grounds of the famous Rose Bowl. On the second Sunday of each month, thousands of people attend this meet, where every item you can imagine is on sale. You name it, someone is selling it! You know the old saying "One person's junk is another's treasure." Items commonly sold are antiques, collectibles, clothing, furniture, plants, paintings, jewelry, toys, and food. Believe me, you can sell anything.

Start-up costs can be low, depending on what you are selling and how you gather items. Space at a swap meet typically costs $25 to $100 per day, and you can either sell on consignment or sell things that you and your friends make. I suggest frequenting swap meets and flea markets to get a sense of what merchandise sells well. I know a woman who buys discontinued or irregular in-line skates very cheaply from a manufacturer and sells them at swap meets for a hefty profit. Then there are those who buy antiques and other goods discounted from estate sales (advertised in the paper) and resell at flea markets.

Swap meets and flea markets are generally open from 7:00 A.M. to 3:00 P.M., and the vendors usually arrive between 6:00 A.M. and 8:00 A.M. You will need to call the flea markets and swap meets you are interested in for specific information and policies. In certain cities you will need a location-specific permit for each swap meet you work at. You can get one for free from the state board of equalization. Call the one nearest you for more information. The *Flea Market Guide of US Flea Markets* has a comprehensive list of flea markets in every state and Canada. On its Web site, www.fleamarketguide.com, you will find the specific hours, the cost of renting a booth, and other valuable information for many swap meets and flea markets.

Income from working at swap meets varies. Earning a few hundred dollars a day profit is not uncommon, and the chance to make a lot of money over a short period of time is a huge incentive for this type of work. Many swap meets and flea markets are available across the country. Check your yellow pages under "Swap Meets" and "Flea Markets." Word of mouth is a great way to learn about hot locations for your items, so when you frequent swap meets, ask vendors which other meets are the best.

Good luck.

- **BENEFITS:** Weekend work; self-employment; meeting people; making a lot of money.
- **PITFALLS:** Earnings vary; early day, long day.
- **SOURCES:** Call swap meets and flea markets for specific information, state board of equalization, yellow pages under "Swap Meets" and "Flea Markets." In California, the Rose Bowl Flea Market and Swap Meet at 323-560-SHOW, www.rgcshows.com/rosebowl.asp; Pasadena City College Flea Market at 626-585-7906, www.paccd.cc.ca.us/stulrnsv/flea/fleahome.htm. In New York City, Garage Antique Shop at 212-647-0707. In the D.C. area, Georgetown Flea Market, 202-223-0289. Other helpful organizations: Na-

tional Flea Market Association, 602-995-3532, www.flea
markets.org; *Flea Market Guide of US Flea Markets*, www.
fleamarketguide.com; National Flea Marketeer, 270-276-
9546, www.fleamarketeer.org.

- **NEEDS:** Product to sell; a permit.

Teaching What You Know

Every person has a talent or ability that can be shared with others—for a fee, of course! The possibilities of what you can teach
are endless: accents/dialects, martial arts, yoga, improvisation,
writing, computer skills, dance, musical instruments, stand-up
routines, on-camera commercial techniques, voice-over workshops, song interpretation, children's theater, magic, photography . . . the list goes on. Think about your talents and hobbies;
make a list; ask your friends; browse through catalogs and
bookstores for ideas. Teaching isn't just for teachers. There are
countless untold stories of ordinary people who apply their
natural skills and abilities to make a good living teaching others. A professional writer I know recently rented a space at
Highways, a cultural arts center in Santa Monica, California,
and taught a successful playwriting workshop. Another friend
teaches a personal finance course at the local adult education
center. You can give private lessons in almost anything, but it
takes a bit of self-promotion. If you prefer a bit more structure,
you can find teaching positions at established schools and
learning institutions by submitting a résumé or class proposal.

You will probably need to advertise for students when form-
ing your own classes. Distributing flyers in your community
and at theaters if you're teaching any sort of acting or writing
technique and advertising in specific trade papers, free local
publications, and featured sections of local papers are great
ways to spread the word. Of course, referrals generally work
best.

Pay will vary. Independent learning institutions, universities, community schools, dance schools, music schools, churches and synagogues, senior centers, and private schools (no state certification needed) will have their own pay scales. If you form your own class or teach privately, check around to keep your rates competitive.

Good luck.

- **BENEFITS:** Substantial income; learning as you teach; contacts.
- **PITFALLS:** Gathering students; teaching what you would rather be doing.
- **SOURCES:** Call institutions about teaching requirements. Advertising.
- **NEEDS:** Patience; good communication skills; more patience.

Video Production Service

If capturing people's most personal, prized, intimate moments and exercising your artistry with a video camera is appealing, then a video production service may be the right job for you. Videographers are hired to videotape a wide range of affairs: weddings, birthdays, anniversaries, bar and bat mitzvahs, reunions, seminars, and theatrical or musical events. The job enables you to attend a variety of functions, meet people, and, if it's your own business, make an excellent hourly wage. Being a videographer is a particularly excellent job for a film student who has access to video equipment. If you're not enrolled in a film school, post a sign at one and hook up with a student. This job is definitely easier and more flexible with two people, especially if the hosts ask you to interview the attendees; one person works the camera while the other walks around with the microphone.

If it's your own business, you'll need to market yourself by advertising in community newsletters, local newspapers and magazines, and trade publications; posting flyers; and advertising at expos (events that focus on specific industries). My husband and I found our wedding videographer at a wedding expo. Alternatively, you may want to work for an existing company where you can start as an assistant to learn the ropes. Check the yellow pages under "Video Production Services."

You can buy or rent equipment, either new or used. Check the yellow pages under "Video Recorders and Players." For certain functions, a final edited video is required. Consider hooking up with a video editor or film school student; such people have access to all the equipment for free and know how to use it. Also, relatively inexpensive and easy-to-use software programs for editing videos, which you can use on a personal computer, are now available. A couple of good products are iMovie for Macs and Ulead VideoStudio for PCs. A new basic digital video camera starts at about $500 to $800, and you can get a new analog video camera for approximately $250 to $400. If you rent a video camera, an analog will be about $50 per day, and a digital approximately $100 a day.

The going rate for a videographer is $100 to $150 per hour. An event such as a wedding will range from $495 to $1,200, depending on hours, experience, and location of the affair. The going rate for video copies is $25 to $35 a tape.

Good luck.

- **BENEFITS:** High hourly wage; creative work.
- **PITFALLS:** Rental fee or initial investment of equipment.
- **SOURCES:** Yellow pages under "Video Production Services." Local magazines and newspapers.
- **NEEDS:** Camera experience; ability to be creative; friendly, professional, reliable attitudes.

- **IDEAS:** A friend in Cleveland told me about a popular video service that records a day in the life. A videographer comes to your home and videotapes your routine with your family and so on. What a terrific idea!

Wedding Coordinator/Event Planner

One of the most significant and pressure-filled events in a family's life is the much-anticipated wedding day. Hiring a wedding coordinator to handle all the details (like making sure Aunt Rose doesn't sit next to Aunt Matilda) can help ensure a smooth event. If you enjoy planning parties, have a knack for design, are resourceful, and can remain calm in stressful situations, consider becoming a wedding coordinator.

It is important to be able to personalize each function. Many wedding coordinators meet at their clients' homes to get a feel for their tastes and styles. A wedding coordinator must be familiar with the many aspects of a wedding: local hotels and wedding sites, catering services, florists, bands, where to rent equipment and order invitations. Wedding coordinators often get special prices, enabling their clients to save money in many of these areas.

Planning a wedding involves many details, and people hire coordinators for different tasks, depending on their budgets. You may be contracted as a full-service coordinator, handling everything and hiring everyone for the affair, or you may be hired to handle last-minute details, including presiding over everything on the day of the event. If you don't have much experience in party planning, it may be a good idea to work in a hotel or catering business for a spell, assisting the director or another upper-level staff member. This is how to make contacts. It is crucial to know the most reliable vendors so that you can give your clients the best prices and services available.

Pay will vary. Call competitors in your area to see what the going rate is. Most wedding coordinators charge flat fees for the affair, which can range from $500 to a few thousand dollars, or 10 percent of the entire cost of the affair. Others work on a consultation basis and are paid an hourly wage, typically $50 to $150 an hour.

To find employment, you need to network. Contacts can be made through organizations, women's groups, bridal shops, churches, and temples. Advertise in local papers or bulletins. Consider getting a booth at a wedding expo, which can be found by contacting editors of bridal magazines or manufacturers of bridal gowns. Build a reputation, and word of mouth will build your business.

Good luck.

- **BENEFITS:** Creative and fun work; organizing a joyous occasion; flexible hours.
- **PITFALLS:** Working under stress; pressure; dealing with nervous parents; being on your feet throughout the affair.
- **SOURCES:** Networking. Advertising. Wedding expos. Bridal shops and magazines.
- **NEEDS:** Artistic background; knowing reliable vendors; even temperament; resourcefulness; being well organized.
- **IDEAS:** Wedding invitations are a lucrative business. You can design and market them yourself or sell them from established catalogs (listed at the backs of bridal magazines). Note that I titled this job "event planner" as well, because there are many business opportunities in planning functions for corporations, bar and bat mitzvahs, sweet-sixteen parties, private parties, and so on.

Yard Sales

All over the country you can find bountiful weekend yard sales. My husband and I have had a few such sales with our old clothes and knickknacks. We've profited a few hundred dollars each time. It's not surprising. Selling used articles inexpensively is a great way to make fast cash! It seems as if every Saturday and Sunday there are front yards filled with everything from furniture to clothing.

There are two ways to profit from yard sales: Sell your own stuff, or buy and resell someone else's. Local papers advertise plenty of estate sales, where quality antiques can be bought and then sold to stores for hefty profits. People who buy out yard and estate sales often do it as a side job. They go early in the morning and buy all the good merchandise for inexpensive prices. Then they go to a higher-income, more crowded area and resell everything at a higher price. On the downside, the income is unsteady, and you need to work constantly to gather items from people and to store the goods between sales.

Good places to sell are high-traffic areas or neighborhoods where people walk around. If you don't live in a busy neighborhood, maybe a friend does. Advertise in community papers (some are free), and post signs in the neighborhood. In some cities, depending on how often you want to participate, a permit may be required.

In this business you'll never want for merchandise. Many people will be happy to give you their "junk" if you come over and haul it away. Consider setting up a business with a friend. You can keep items in your garage or attic if storage is a problem. Another option is to rent a garage or a self-storage space. The nationwide chain U Store-it is one such company, and a five-by-ten space about the size of a large walk-in closet, costs from $65 to $140 per month. Prices vary a lot, depending on whether you get the storage in a major city or a more rural area. Income will vary with what you are selling and where. Higher-income neighborhoods yield higher profits.

Good luck.

- **BENEFITS:** Immediate cash; flexible hours; weekend work.
- **PITFALLS:** Unsteady income; need to gather and store the goods.
- **SOURCES:** Local papers. Driving or walking around neighborhoods. Advertising your services. Posting signs.
- **NEEDS:** Items to sell; place to sell them; storage area; truck or large car.

2

Nine to Five . . . Not

PICK A SHIFT THAT WORKS FOR YOU

Advertising Sales Representative

Bet you never guessed that you could turn your enthusiasm for a weekly publication or magazine into a part-time job. Are you a mom or dad who enjoys reading parent magazines? Or a vegetarian who reads *Vegetarian Times* and other health-conscious publications? However passionate you may be about the subject or articles, the heart of every magazine is in the advertisements. Ads are what keep the magazine afloat, and publishers often hire outside people to scout for new ones.

Energetic, creative, and naturally organized people are well suited for this job. Basically, you scout businesses that have placed ads in other publications and try to convince them to advertise in your magazine, and you approach new businesses. You meet the person interested in placing the ad, help create the size and style, knowing what works best in your particular magazine, and send it to the office of the company you work for, which handles the rest. Most of the work is typically done from your home, where you can have separate phone lines installed or two lines on the same phone. For many local magazines and papers, knowing your neighborhood and potential clients who will place ads is helpful.

Salary is usually commission-based, normally 15 to 20 percent of sales. Advertising sales reps in major cities earn an average of $10 to $18 an hour. The potential for earnings is generally based on the time invested.

To obtain a sales rep position, simply contact weekly publications, newspapers, or magazines you are interested in working for. Radio and TV stations also hire advertising sales reps. A background in sales is beneficial.

Good luck.

- **BENEFITS:** Flexible workdays; creating your own hours; working from home.
- **PITFALLS:** Fluctuating salary.
- **SOURCES:** Contact human resources at newspapers, magazines, TV and radio stations.
- **NEEDS:** High energy; creativity; enthusiasm; enjoyment of working in sales.

Airport Shuttle Service

Necessity is the mother of invention. For years people wanted a quick, easy way to get to the airport without paying the high costs of a taxi or limousine. Enter the airport shuttle service or, as the industry calls it, the share ride business.

You may work for a number of companies that offer this service. Most, like the furiously franchising Super Shuttle, require a minimum three-day workweek. Shifts are usually ten hours, with a number of shifts available since service is offered twenty-four hours a day in major cities. Basically, once you check out the van from the company you work for, you're on your own, meaning there is no boss looking over your shoulder, and your earnings will depend on how many passengers you pick up. You must be at least twenty-one years of age and have a clean driving record. When hired, you will receive one week of training at minimum-wage salary. The standard uniform consists of black pants, white shirt, and black tie.

Pay is commission-based when you work at smaller companies. Expect to earn 25 to 30 percent of the gross revenue of the van. Cash tips are your own. Larger companies usually pay hourly rates, and you can typically earn up to $18 an hour plus tips. To apply for a job, look in the yellow pages under "Airport Transportation Service."

A last note: Rental car companies need drivers to take people to and from the rental car agency and the airport. For employment opportunities, look in the yellow pages under "Automobile Renting."

Good luck.

- **BENEFITS:** Availability of different shifts; being unsupervised.
- **PITFALLS:** Within your assigned schedule there is not much flexibility; driving can be exhausting.
- **SOURCES:** Any shuttle service at airport. For Super Shuttle, call 800-BLUE-VAN, www.supershuttle.com. A few well-known rental companies are Enterprise, 800-325-8007, www.enterprise.com; Alamo, 800-GO-ALAMO, www.alamo.com; Avis, 800-831-2847, www.avis.com; Hertz, 800-654-3131, www.hertz.com.
- **NEEDS:** Love of driving.

Casino Jobs

The thrill, the rush, the tumult, the "flush": If these words pique your interest, working in a casino may be the perfect job for you. From the shores of New Jersey to the Rocky Mountains to the glitzy desert oasis of Las Vegas, casino establishments now exist in more than thirty-four states. These gambling paradises frequented by high rollers hoping to make some quick cash are usually open twenty-four hours a day, seven days a week, meaning that you can select from a number of round-the-clock shifts. Casinos provide part-time employment opportunities, such as slot cashiers, cocktail servers, dealers, and casino surveillance personnel.

SLOT CASHIER

Slot cashiers, often called cage cashiers, assist customers in making change, exchanging cash, and running credit card transactions for chips. You need to be at least eighteen years of age, preferably with cashier experience. Expect to earn anywhere from $7 to $12 an hour.

COCKTAIL SERVER

Cocktail servers are often required to have a minimum of two years of cocktail or waiter experience. At the time of your interview, you may be quizzed on the contents of different alcoholic drinks. If you want to boost your bartending marketability, there are a number of books to read on mixed drinks. Two popular ones are *Mr. Boston's Official Bartending and Party Guide*, published by Warner Books, and *The Original Guide to American Cocktails and Drinks*, published by Bar Media. Cocktail servers usually make minimum wage plus tips.

DEALER

Dealers are generally required to have been to some type of gaming school. In Atlantic City the Casino Career Institute has trained more than forty-six thousand students since 1978. Most houses require you to be proficient at a minimum of two games, usually blackjack and a choice of craps, poker, baccarat, roulette, minibaccarat, pai gow poker, or pai gow tiles. Many locations ask that you have a casino license. In New Jersey a casino license costs $350 and is good for three years. Call the New Jersey Casino Control Commission for more information. Dealers are generally paid minimum wage plus tips. Expect to earn $25,000 to $35,000 a year part-time.

SURVEILLANCE WORKER

A surveillance job involves monitoring the games, players, and employees. You are basically an "eye in the sky." In other words, you are hired to protect the casino's assets. You sit in a room with several television monitors and scan the bars, restaurants, and gambling floors. VCRs record the game and bar areas at all times, and you must make certain that the tapes are working and set up for the next shift. If an unusual situation or a discrepancy comes up, you are required to review the video and write a report on what happened. There are three shifts available at most casinos: 6:00 A.M. to 2:00 P.M., 2:00 P.M. to 10:00 P.M., and 10:00 P.M. to 6:00 A.M. You are typically scheduled for five shifts a week. You may feel isolated from the hubbub of the casino, but you can listen to music and read in between scanning. The salary usually ranges from $11.25 to $17 an hour.

For employment opportunities, check the yellow pages under "Casinos" or use your Web browser—for example, Netscape or Internet Explorer—and choose one of the many search engines available, such as Google, Yahoo, or Infoseek, and type in "Casino." Note: A couple of books to assist in finding casinos in your area are *Casinos: The International Casino Guide*, published by BDIT, and *American Casino Guide*, by Steve Bourie.

Good luck.

- **BENEFITS:** Steady salary; flexible shifts.
- **PITFALLS:** Gambling away your salary; noisy, smoke-filled, crowded environment (granted, that might be a benefit for some).
- **SOURCES:** Yellow pages under "Casinos." *Casinos: The In-*

ternational Casino Guide, published by BDIT, 800-257-5344. *American Casino Guide*, by Steve Bourie. Casino Career Institute, 609-343-4848, www.atlantic.edu/casino. New Jersey Casino Control Commission (CCC), 609-441-3749, www.state.nj.us/casinos. In California three popular casinos are the Bicycle Club Casino, 562-806-4646, www.thebicyclecasino.com; the Hollywood Park, 310-330-2800, www.playhpc.com; and the Commerce Casino, 213-721-2100. The Foxwoods Casino, 800-FOXWOODS, 866-4FOXJOB, www.foxwoods.com, in Connecticut, is very popular for the Boston, Providence, and overall New England area. In New Jersey, try any of the casinos in Atlantic City. The *Press of Atlantic City* will have many job listings, www.pressofatlanticcity.com. Tropicana Casino & Resort, 800-843-8767, is a good one. For a list of hotels/casinos in Las Vegas, contact the Commission on Economic Development at 702-687-4325. CasinoGuide, www.casinoguide.ws/usa.html.

• **NEEDS:** Knowledge of casino games; some casinos require a gaming school certificate.

Catering

My friend Allison attended the Oscars this past year, and she wasn't even nominated! How'd she do it? She worked for the Ambrosia Company, an upscale catering and event-planning business in Los Angeles. Caterers are hired for a wide range of affairs; intimate dinner parties, weddings, bar and bat mitzvahs, film and TV wrap parties (for the cast and crew), as well as gala social and political events.

If you work for a caterer, your responsibilities may include unloading trucks, setting up tables and chairs, setting tables and cocktail areas, prepping and serving food, busing tables, bartending, cleaning up, and then reloading the entire shebang on the trucks to return to the office. It is important to have a professional attitude and show up on time with a neat, clean appearance. A black tuxedo uniform is essential. I suggest going to a vintage store to look for a used tuxedo: single-breasted black jacket, wing-tipped tux shirt, and black bow tie and cummerbund. On the job, French service know-how is helpful and sometimes necessary. The basics of French service consist of holding a platter of food in your left hand while serving individual food items from utensils in your right hand and of always serving from the left and clearing from the right (except for beverages, which are always served from the right). Most caterers will want you to have experience in the food industry.

Catering hours are flexible, usually at night and on the weekend. Around the winter holiday season the business flourishes, so it is a great time to work hard and save extra dollars for the slower months. The best part of catering, the reason so many people prefer it to restaurant work, is the variety. Catered events are often held in places like museums and theaters for receptions, giant halls for functions, and private homes for big and small parties alike. Also, as we've seen, it can be a great way to attend the Oscars or Grammys!

Catering companies typically pay $8 to $18 per hour, depending on your experience and the city you live in, with a four- or five-hour guarantee. This means that if the party goes for only an hour and a half, you still get paid for the guaranteed time. Many times, at the end of the night, you will be tipped by the host of the party, but don't expect a tip every time.

There are hundreds of catering companies, and once you begin catering, you'll be able to network and find out which are the better companies to work for. Many companies contract out people to help in the kitchen, serve food, or bartend. One company in Los Angeles called Host Helper will hire you as an independent contractor. This means that the host pays you directly, and you then pay Host Helper a placement fee. It considers itself a marketing arm for people on its registry. For other similar employment opportunities in your city, look in the yellow pages under "Caterers," "Party Service," and "Employment Agencies."

Good luck.

- **BENEFITS:** Good salary; varied and interesting locations.
- **PITFALLS:** Having to stand on your feet; physically demanding; unsteady work.
- **SOURCES:** Yellow pages under "Caterers," "Party Service," and "Employment Agencies." In Los Angeles, call Host Helpers, 310-475-8100, and Party Staff, 323-933-3900. In New York, call For Your Occasion, Inc., 917-441-0461. In the D.C. area, call Federal City Caterers, 202-408-9700, www.federalcity.com. In Chicago, get in touch with Gaper's Caterers, 312-787-5173, www.culinaryenterprises. com, or use a search engine such as Google on the Internet to check for local caterers.
- **NEEDS:** Restaurant or food experience; a black tuxedo uniform.

Club Work

The days of Studio 54 and the Limelight are over, but nightclubs are alive and well, still beckoning the hip, the trendy, and the retro-funky to their doors. And for you nocturnal neophytes, working in a club may be the right gig.

On one hand, club work enables you to meet a lot of people, listen to good music, and be part of the scene. People are out having fun and spending money freely. On the other hand, you will be dealing with smoke-filled rooms, late hours, and loud music. If this is not for you, then working in a restaurant or a low-key lounge may be a better idea. To get a job in a club, check the yellow pages under "Clubs and Cocktail Lounges." Ask your friends or people in music stores to recommend some hot spots, and look at the local community paper or the entertainment section of your newspaper for listings of popular hangouts. The main jobs available are bartender, waiter, cocktail waiter, and bouncer/doorman.

BARTENDER

Sex on the beach, kamikaze, and fuzzy navel. No, this is not a list of activities you engaged in when you graduated from college. These are just three of the mixed drinks you'll need to know as a bartender. A bartender's duties include setting up the bar, stocking beverages, maintaining an inventory of items, cutting fruit for the condiment tray, cleaning glassware, and mixing drinks for bar customers and the wait staff. The hours tend to be later in a club than in a restaurant, often until dawn. Many clubs don't even open until nighttime. Still, bartenders at popular clubs can make $200 a night or more. If you presently lack bartending experience and knowledge of mixed drinks, sign up for a reputable bartending course. Schools usually charge between $300 and $500 for the course, with scholarships and creative financing available. Many schools will help place you in jobs upon completion. A few reputable ones are the National Bartenders School, American Bartenders School, and Professional Bartending School of New England. Two reliable books on mixed drinks are *Mr. Boston's Official Bartending Guide*, published by Warner Books, and *The Original Guide to American Cocktails and Drinks*, published by Bar Media.

WAITER/WAITRESS

Where can you still get great tips, always be well fed, listen to hip music while you work, and develop your leg muscles? That old standby serving food is still one of the most popular part-time, flexible ways to earn a great wage. Waiting tables in a nightclub offers an added element of excitement. Once again, the hours are a lot later, and the dress code may differ. The wages tend to be higher if the shift is longer . . . and the skirt is shorter.

A waiter's job is to take food and drink orders, serve the requested items, and tend to customer needs. Side work involves setting up tables, refilling condiments, polishing glasses and silver, and cleaning counters and work areas. It is important to be efficient and personable. Having a good memory is definitely an asset since you will need to know and recite the daily specials. Sometimes a more extensive knowledge of wine and food is required.

The positive aspects of being a waiter are fast access to cash, flexible schedules, and free meals. The hours vary, depending on the club and your shift assignment. On the downside, you'll have to work at a frantic pace during peak hours and put up with sometimes erratic income; poor tips can alter your mood pretty darn fast. Salary consists of minimum wage plus tips. Tips will vary according on the location and size of the club. An average dinner shift in a mid-size club in a major city pays $100 a night.

Before accepting a job at a club or even applying for one, try to gauge the volume of customers as well as the prices on the menu; tips are commensurate with these factors. To get started, look in the help wanted section of the newspaper, ask friends, or apply at clubs during slow evenings, Sunday to Tuesday at off-peak times (between 3:00 P.M. and 5:00 P.M.).

COCKTAIL WAITER/WAITRESS

Cocktail waiting is similar to regular waiting, except you are primarily serving drinks instead of food. Unlike the waiter at a restaurant, the cocktail waiter at a club rarely deals with the kitchen.

You start the evening with a bank (a belt pack with money broken down into change for the evening), and you do all your money transactions directly with the customer. You pay the bar directly out of your personal bank, and the customer reimburses you. If a customer pays by credit card, you must run a copy of the card before delivering drinks to ensure payment just in case the customer gets the sudden urge to walk out. Although it's a change of pace from regular restaurant work, the whole system is simple once you learn it.

Unlike other restaurant or club jobs, the waiter does not need to come in as soon as the establishment opens but can arrive just before the busy period and leave when the crowd dies down. A good cocktail position in a busy club can be quite lucrative, with relatively short hours. Even today, with all the hype about sexual discrimination, most clubs prefer to hire attractive, sexy women as cocktail waitresses (shocking, isn't it?).

To find a job, look in the yellow pages under "Clubs and Cocktail Lounges," ask around, and check out the music and entertainment sections of local papers for the names of popular clubs. You might try asking people who work in music stores since they often know the hot spots. Salary varies greatly, usually from $80 to $200 a night, depending on the shift, tipping system (pooling or keeping your own), location, and popularity of club.

BOUNCER/DOORMAN

A bouncer's job is primarily to check IDs so that minors don't slip in and to protect club workers and patrons. A bouncer helps establish a pleasant and safe environment so that people can come and have a good time.

Hours are flexible. Bouncing is a nighttime gig, starting anywhere between 6:00 P.M. and 11:00 P.M. and lasting until about 2:00 A.M. You can work just a few nights a week or more if you prefer. Typically one or two bouncers will come in early for happy hour, and then another will arrive every hour or so. By 11:00 P.M. the club should be fully staffed with about ten to eleven bouncers working each night. Benefits include decent pay, meeting a lot of people, making connections, and being "tipped" with phone numbers (whoo-haa). On the negative side, it can become dangerous if people get angry when refused entrance or become drunk and out of control.

To be a bouncer, you need to speak English and communicate effectively. It helps to look intimidating, be in great physical shape, and know a form of martial arts. Usually male bouncers are preferred. The pay is $9 to $15 an hour, depending on experience and duration of employment at a particular club.

To get a job as a bouncer or doorman, go through anyone you know who works at a club. Word of mouth and personal referrals are the best means to secure a job of this kind. Check out your paper's entertainment section for names of popular night spots, or look in the yellow pages under "Clubs."

Good luck.

- **BENEFITS:** Meeting people; making connections; having days free; good money; listening to music.
- **PITFALLS:** Smoke-filled rooms; loud music; late hours; having to stand on your feet for long hours.
- **SOURCES:** Word of mouth. Yellow pages under "Clubs." Na-

tional Bartenders School, 800-646-MIXX, www.national
bartenders.com; American Bartenders School, 800-736-
1001, www.barbook.com; Professional Bartending School
of New England, in New England itself, 781-646-9900,
from outside New England, call 888-437-4657, www.
bartendingschool.com/NewEngland; New York Bartending School, 212-768-8460, www.newyorkbartending
school.com. American Bartenders' Association, 800-935-
3232, www.americanbartenders.org. Two reliable books
on mixed drinks are *Mr. Boston's Official Bartending Guide*,
published by Warner Books, and *The Original Guide to
American Cocktails and Drinks*, published by Bar Media.
Check local bookstores or Amazon.com.

- **NEEDS:** Restaurant or club experience preferred; for
bouncer position, looking intimidating, knowing martial
arts (or at least how to break up a fight!).

Coffeehouses

The sentence "Let's go get a cup of coffee" has taken on a whole
new meaning since the nineties. Today coffeehouses are vibrant,
sometimes kitschy places where young Kafka readers and caf-
feine junkies go to schmooze. These eclectic places offer job
hunters a social atmosphere and flexible hours, with both full-
and part-time shifts available. To become a behind-the-counter
worker, a *barista*, you must have an interest in coffee, be willing
to stand 90 percent of the time, and be quick on your feet.

You can work at the trendy little coffeehouse around the cor-
ner or at one of the national chains, such as Starbucks. Store
hours for Starbucks vary, depending on location, although
many are open from 6:30 A.M. to 11:00 P.M. Starbucks provides
five days of training, approximately twenty-four hours total.
You will learn all you need to know about coffee, tea, equipment, and general procedures.

The best way to get a job at a coffeehouse is to apply when a manager is in the store since personal meetings are always best. Ask around for names of popular coffeehouses, or check the yellow pages under "Coffee Dealers—Retail." To work at Starbucks or another franchise, call information for locations in your area.

The salary starts at about $8 an hour. In many coffeehouses where you serve people, you'll also make tips. At Starbucks a minimum of twenty hours a week entitles you to full health and dental benefits. In addition, a twenty-hour workweek allows you the option of a 401K retirement plan. Employees are even entitled to buy discounted stock in the company.

Good luck.

- **BENEFITS:** Social atmosphere; flexible shifts; comprehensive benefits.
- **PITFALLS:** Having to be on your feet; very physical work.
- **SOURCES:** Call information for Starbucks in your area or visit www.starbucks.com. Check yellow pages under "Coffee Dealers—Retail."
- **NEEDS:** Being quick on your feet; having an interest in coffee.

Delivering Food for Restaurants

From Joe's Diner to your local five-star restaurant, food establishments everywhere are now jumping on the delivery bandwagon. Delivering food for restaurants and pizza joints is a terrific way to make quick cash. As a delivery person you work as an independent contractor; there is no boss hovering over you, and you can listen to music or books on tape while making money. Your car will experience wear and tear, and being called the pizza boy or pizza girl might cause you to cringe, but the benefits far outweigh the disadvantages.

Shifts are typically four to six hours, with both nighttime shifts and day shifts available. This job is flexible in that you arrange your own schedule, and in many cases, you can switch a shift if need be.

To qualify to work this job, you need a car and insurance (in New York City, a bike, the subway, or your feet will do the job). Knowledge of the area where you will be working, which can easily be acquired with a good map, is preferred. Your time is spent in your automobile, so air-conditioning is helpful. The pay is typically minimum wage plus tips, or $3 per delivery plus tips. The average income from working a five-hour shift at a mid-size restaurant is about $75.

For specific jobs, check the classified section under "Drivers" or "Restaurants" or the yellow pages under "Restaurants," or inquire at any restaurant or pizza place that provides delivery. Services that deliver from a catalog of local restaurants are popping up in most major cities. Dining In is one such company that has delivery services in Boston, Chicago, Dallas, and Philadelphia. If you have the entrepreneurial spirit, consider starting your own.

Good luck.

- **BENEFITS:** Flexible work hours; no boss around; can listen to music or books on tape in your car.
- **PITFALLS:** Wear and tear on your car.
- **SOURCES:** Restaurants that deliver (check yellow pages). Classifieds. Telephone Dining In—Boston, 617-783-0777; Chicago, 312-491-1999; Dallas, 972-732-1686; and Philadelphia, 215-574-1600—or visit its Web site at www.diningin.com.
- **NEEDS:** Working knowledge of the area; a car and car insurance in most cities.

Directory Assistance Operator

Directory assistance operators find phone listings and addresses for callers. This job is actually pretty much a full-time position, as employees are expected to work 32½ to 37½ hours a week. I include it here because split shifts are available, meaning that you can come in for four hours in the morning and then back for four hours in the evening if you like. Some "stations" are open twenty-four hours a day and others from 7:00 A.M. to 11:00 P.M. A phone bar (an area with usable phones) is accessible to workers during their breaks, allowing them free calls within surrounding counties. There are generally periodic breaks allowed every few hours. Directory assistance operators must be on time for their shifts, have good customer service skills, be courteous to callers, and be available to work a variety of hours. When you are hired, you will be required to take a weeklong crash course that teaches you everything you'll need to know for the job. Keep in mind, this is a sedentary position and is not a wise choice for anyone who likes to move around. You have to be on the phone for at least two hours at a time. Of course, many of you phone junkies won't have a problem with this requirement.

Pay typically starts at $8 to $9 an hour. Excellent health benefits, including dental and eye insurance, are provided. For more information, call your local phone company.

Good luck.

- **BENEFITS:** Steady income; excellent health benefits; varied shifts and split shifts.
- **PITFALLS:** Must work 37½ hours a week; rude customers.
- **SOURCES:** Your local phone company.
- **NEEDS:** Customer service experience; ability to work various hours and split shifts.

Hotel Jobs

Hotels offer a number of flexible, part-time employment opportunities, including bellhop, concierge, doorman, front desk clerk, and room service waiter. Keep in mind when applying for hotel positions that there are advantages to working at larger, more expensive hotels. Above all, you will make more money, and trading shifts is easier since there are more employees.

BELLHOP

The bellhop's duties include greeting guests, carrying their bags, escorting people to their rooms, showing the facilities in the rooms, handling storage of bags, and tending to customers who may have special requests. In hotels that do not have a room service department, the bellhop is responsible for ice, making trips to a store if necessary, and bringing requested items up to the rooms. One perk is that you get to meet people from all over the world.

The bellhop must have a courteous demeanor and a neat appearance. Also, a good working knowledge of spots around town is helpful since guests unfamiliar with the area will often ask questions. The hours vary. Shifts are usually 7:00 A.M. to 3:00 P.M., 3:00 P.M. to 11:00 P.M., and 11:00 P.M. to 7:00 A.M. Note that during the graveyard shift, people do not travel as much, and therefore, tips tend to be scarce.

Most hotels pay $7 to $10 an hour plus tips from guests. In an upscale hotel a bellhop can make about $800 per week. Group tours have a preset price paid per person for bellhop services. Most hotels offer comprehensive health benefits.

For a complete listing of hotels in your area, check your yellow pages. A few national upscale hotel chains are Nikko, Four Seasons, Biltmore, and Marriott.

Good luck.

- **BENEFITS:** Steady salary plus tips; meeting people from around the world.
- **PITFALLS:** Physical labor; polyester uniform can be hot during the summer.
- **SOURCES:** Yellow pages under "Hotels." Nikko, 800-NIKKO US, www.nikkohotels.com. Marriott, 888-4MARRIOTT, www.marriott.com. For the Four Seasons, the Biltmore, or other chains, contact its nearest hotel directly.
- **NEEDS:** Working knowledge of spots around town; neatness and courtesy.

CONCIERGE

The job of the concierge is pivotal in a hotel. Guests look to the concierge not only for hospitality but for problem solving. He or she informs guests about the city, suggesting restaurants, attractions, and places of interest, cautions people about areas to avoid, and makes restaurant and ticket reservations. At some hotels the concierge also handles currency exchange. As a result, the concierge must have strong communication skills to deal with hotel guests and make arrangements with vendors outside the hotel. Extensive knowledge of the city is also important. Many hotels with international clienteles prefer to hire a person who is fluent in one or more foreign languages.

Typical shifts are 7:00 A.M. to 3:00 P.M., 3:00 P.M. to 11:00 P.M., and 11:00 P.M. to 7:00 A.M. The flexibility factor can be a bit tougher with this particular position. Many hotels do have other personnel who can double as concierge, but your ability to switch shifts often depends on the willingness of your coworkers and the rules of the hotel. A terrific benefit of this job is the opportunity to make contacts all over town. On the downside, dealing with the public can be frustrating, and the concierge can often be the brunt of complaints on all levels. A concierge can expect to make up to $15 an hour plus tips. Rest assured that the ability to get a reservation or secure a spot at a sold-out event does not go unrewarded. Most hotels offer comprehensive health benefits.

For a complete listing of hotels in your area, check the local yellow pages. A few national upscale hotel chains are Nikko, Four Seasons, Biltmore, and Marriott.

Good luck.

- **BENEFITS:** Steady salary plus tips; making contacts all over town.
- **PITFALLS:** Having to deal with complaints.
- **SOURCES:** Yellow pages under "Hotels." Nikko, 800-NIKKO US, www.nikkohotels.com. Marriott, 888-4MARRIOTT, www.marriott.com. For the Four Seasons, the Biltmore, or other chains, contact its nearest hotel directly.
- **NEEDS:** friendliness; neat appearance; ability to schmooze; working knowledge of the city; fluency in foreign languages is helpful.

DOORMAN

The doorman of a hotel greets hotel patrons when they arrive, helps them out of their cabs or assists in handling valet parking, directs them to the check-in area, and opens the door when they enter or leave. A hotel doorman must be friendly, neat in appearance, and knowledgeable about the city.

This job offers the opportunity to work outside, so you are not under the constant scrutiny of others. There is no "head doorman," so there is a certain freedom attached to this position. Unfortunately, working outside also means exposure to inclement weather. Unless *Singin' in the Rain* is your favorite musical, this can be unpleasant. The hours are usually standard hotel shifts: 7:00 A.M. to 3:00 P.M., 3:00 P.M. to 11:00 P.M., and 11:00 P.M. to 7:00 A.M. The shifts can be switched depending on coworkers' availability. During the 11:00 P.M. to 7:00 A.M. shift you won't have to work as hard, but you will also receive few or no tips. The salary is about $8 to $15 an hour, and most hotels offer comprehensive health benefits. With tips this job can be extremely lucrative. The doorman will often get tipped both when the customer arrives at and departs from the hotel. A doorman at a busy hotel can earn in excess of $500 per week in tips.

For hotel listings, check the yellow pages under "Hotels." A few national upscale hotel chains are Nikko, Four Seasons, Biltmore, and Marriott.

Good luck.

- **BENEFITS:** Steady salary plus tips; working outside.
- **PITFALLS:** Having to stand at all times; exposure to inclement weather; opening and closing the door again and again and again . . .
- **SOURCES:** Yellow pages under "Hotels." Nikko, 800-NIKKO US, www.nikkohotels.com. Marriott, 888-4MARRIOTT, www.marriott.com. For the Four Seasons, the Biltmore, or other chains, contact its nearest hotel directly.
- **NEEDS:** friendliness; neat appearance; knowledge of the city.

FRONT DESK CLERK

The front desk clerk is responsible for booking hotel reservations and making sure they are accurate upon the guests' arrival. His or her main objective is to ensure that the guest's stay is as pleasant as possible. The front desk clerk confirms that the room is ready at check-in, deals with any questions or problems the guest may have during his or her stay, and handles checkout. The front desk clerk is responsible for being aware of vacancies at the hotel at any given time, as well as monitoring the duration of a guest's stay and the charges incurred while at the hotel. The front desk clerk also polices in-hotel activities, checking on room availability from housekeeping, making certain guests check out at the appropriate time, and silencing noisy visitors.

This is a job where courtesy is of the utmost importance. As a front desk clerk you are usually the first person with whom a guest makes contact inside the hotel. It is important to have a neat appearance and useful to have an extensive knowledge of the city. Foreign language skills are helpful and sometimes required.

Standard hotel shifts are 7:00 A.M. to 3:00 P.M., 3:00 P.M. to 11:00 P.M., and 11:00 P.M. to 7:00 A.M. Hotels often hire people with accounting or night audit skills to work the graveyard shift and balance the day receipts. Flexibility of shifts varies and usually depends on your peers' willingness to cover. On the downside, you will spend your shift standing; you are dealing with the public (pretty scary sometimes!); and you can be besieged by a guest for any reason whatsoever, even a spider in a room.

Most major chains offer consistent salaries and benefits. If you work for a national or international hotel chain, you will usually receive a sizable discount or a complimentary stay at the hotel you work for and its affiliates. Salary typically ranges from $8 to $12 per hour. If night audit is incorporated, the salary will be higher. The front desk clerk usually does not receive tips.

For hotel listings, check the yellow pages under "Hotels." A few national upscale hotel chains are Nikko, Four Seasons, Biltmore, and Marriott.

Good luck.

- **BENEFITS:** Steady salary; hotel discounts.
- **PITFALLS:** No tips; having to stay on your feet; dealing with demanding guests.

- **SOURCES:** Check the yellow pages under "Hotels." Nikko, 800-NIKKO US, www.nikkohotels.com. Marriott, 888-4MARRIOTT, www.marriott.com. For the Four Seasons, the Biltmore, or other chains, contact its nearest hotel directly.
- **NEEDS:** Neatness and courtesy; responsible attitude; working knowledge of the city. Foreign language skills are helpful.

ROOM SERVICE WAITER

A hotel room service waiter is the person who delivers meals to a guest's room. When the hotel is full, the room service waiter may deliver hundreds of meals a day. It is important to be neat, clean, and in good physical condition because this job entails extensive walking. The hours are standard hotel shifts, 7:00 A.M. to 3:00 P.M., 3:00 P.M. to 11:00 P.M., and 11:00 P.M. to 7:00 A.M., with the exception of the breakfast shift, when the waiter may be required to come in earlier. This is a fairly flexible job as long as your coworkers are willing to trade shifts with you.

This job typically pays between $6 and $10 an hour plus tips. In a large hotel a room service waiter can make a good deal of money for the hours worked. Unfortunately, there is no guarantee of a tip each time you deliver.

For hotel listings in your area, check the yellow pages under "Hotels." A few national upscale hotel chains are Nikko, Four Seasons, Biltmore, and Marriott.

Good luck.

- **BENEFITS:** Steady salary plus tips; flexible shifts.
- **PITFALLS:** A lot of walking with deliveries; no guarantee of tips.
- **SOURCES:** Yellow pages under "Hotels." Nikko, 800-

NIKKO US, www.nikkohotels.com. Marriott, 888-4MARRIOTT, www.marriott.com. For the Four Seasons, the Biltmore, or other chains, contact its nearest hotel directly.

- **NEEDS:** neatness; cleanliness; efficiency; friendliness; good physical condition.

Limousine Driver/Chauffeur

A limo driver transports passengers to and from their destinations in a luxurious vehicle. I have decided to write about limousine rather than taxi driving because the consensus is that this is a safer, more pleasant job. The people I interviewed tended to be limo drivers or chauffeurs for specific celebrities, but there are plenty who cater to the public at large.

To qualify to be a limo driver, you need to be twenty-five years of age or older and have a clean driving record, a driver's license from the state where you plan to drive, and an extensive knowledge of the area. Job flexibility will depend on which company you work for and the schedule you are given. As long as you are responsible and a good driver, most companies are willing to work with your scheduling needs. To get in with a solid, small company that has a select clientele, you first need to pay your dues by working for one of the larger companies. When you begin, be prepared to work long, odd hours. Starting salary is customarily minimum wage plus tips. Once you begin work, you will be able to schmooze with other drivers to find out which companies are the best to work for. After learning the ropes, you can even start your own business.

The yellow pages lists many companies under "Limousine Services" and "Employment Agencies—Domestic Help." Check the classifieds under "Chauffeur." A few nationwide services are Carey Worldwide Chauffeured Services, Limo USA, and Thomas

Transportation. One large limousine company in Los Angeles is Music Express. In Chicago, try Limousine Network and Limos R Us, and in Boston, try Cooper's Limousine.

Good luck.

- **BENEFITS:** You can work off-hours; steady pay.
- **PITFALLS:** Odd hours; long hours; proms; dealing with drunks.
- **SOURCES:** Yellow pages under "Limousine Services" and "Employment Agencies—Domestic Help." Classifieds under "Chauffeur." Carey Worldwide Chauffeured Services, 800-336-4646 or 800-585-9333, www.ecarey.com. Limo USA, 800-451-3011; Thomas Transportation, 800-526-8143, www.thomastransportation.com. Music Express, 323-849-2244. Chicago: Limousine Network, 708-430-0023; Limos R Us, 773-792-9380. Boston: Cooper's Limousine, 617-482-1000.
- **NEEDS:** Must be twenty-five or older; driver's license from the state you'll be driving in; clean driving record; extensive knowledge of the area; good sense of direction.

Market Research

Market research solicits and compiles consumer opinions on products as varied as a new television program to choice of coffees, detergents, toilet papers, cars, and even financial investments. There are basically three flexible jobs available: focus groups, outside recruiters, and phone room recruiters.

FOCUS GROUPS

Focus groups typically involve six to ten men or women who get together in a group setting and give their opinions on products and television shows. There are even "mock jury" focus groups. Being part of a focus group can be a fun and interesting way to make extra money. Since you are allowed to participate in a focus group only once every three to six months per company, the money is not steady. But not to worry, there are plenty of companies to register with and recruiters to contact. At the very least, it is a nice supplemental income.

To participate in a focus group, you first need to qualify. Ethnicity, demographics, age, occupation, and product use will determine participation in a particular group. Manufacturers prefer a balanced sampling of opinions for their criteria. When you call to register, you will be required to answer a list of pre-screening questions. When you are contacted to participate in an actual focus group, you will be screened with specific product questions. Upon qualifying, you'll be given a time and place to show up for the group session. The jobs last from one to a few hours. Occasionally you will be asked to pick up the new product beforehand, try it at home, and answer questions about it. When you have completed and delivered the questionnaire, you will be paid. Pay varies: typically, from $40 to $100 per job. The good news is that it is considered a cash gift, so it doesn't go on your taxes.

For employment opportunities, look in the yellow pages under "Market Research." You will need to call and request to be part of an upcoming research group. Plaza Research, a well-respected market research company, has offices in New York, Los Angeles, Chicago, Denver, Dallas, Atlanta, Philadelphia, Houston, Phoenix, Tampa, Fort Lauderdale, and San Francisco. The Focus Network has offices in Dallas, Chicago, Los Angeles, New York, Atlanta, Toronto, and other international locations. There are many local research centers as well. When you begin participating in focus groups, you'll meet people who know recruiters, who may lead to more work.

Good luck.

- **BENEFITS:** Easy and fun work; quick cash; you become the voice of the masses.
- **PITFALLS:** Unsteady work; may have to drive far.
- **SOURCES:** "Market Research" in yellow pages. Plaza Research, 800-654-8002, www.plazaresearch.com. Focus Network, www.thefocusnetwork.com. Dallas, 800-336-1417; Chicago, 312-951-1616; Los Angeles, 818-501-4794; New York, 212-867-6700; Atlanta, 404-636-9054; Toronto, 416-221-9450.
- **NEEDS:** Transportation to site.

OUTSIDE RECRUITER

Many market research firms employ recruiters to bring in participants for their focus groups. Once an assignment is completed, you bill the firm on the basis of how many of your recruits have shown up. This is a terrific job for an assertive individual with good coordinating skills. A sizable database of contacts is invaluable. Flexibility is a big plus with this job; you work out of your home, at your own pace. Be aware that there are deadlines, though. Each company will provide you with the structure and guidelines you need to follow.

Pay varies depending on the company you work with. The typical range is $15-$30 a head. The average is ten people for each group. For more information, contact market research groups listed in the business-to-business yellow pages and those listed above under "Focus Groups." A few companies that hire outside recruiters in Los Angeles are Adept Consumer Testing and IPSOS-ASI.

Good luck.

- **BENEFITS:** Flexible hours; working at home; good wages.
- **PITFALLS:** Challenge to break into; always being at home with your work.

- **SOURCES:** Yellow pages under "Market Research." Adept Consumer Testing, www.giveusyouropinions.com, 818-905-1525. IPSOS-ASI, www.ipsos-asi.com, Chicago, 773-871-4020, Cincinnati, 513-552-1100, and other locations in the United States and Canada.
- **NEEDS:** Database of names; coordinating ability.

PHONE ROOM RECRUITER

Many market research groups hire people to work in what is called a phone room. There you recruit individuals from specific lists to participate in focus groups. Unlike telemarketing, you are not selling anything. You are simply inviting people to participate in a group discussion so that they can make money. This is an appropriate job for anyone who is outgoing and friendly and enjoys phone work. Flexible shifts are available. The late-in-the-day 5:00 P.M. to 9:00 P.M. shift is popular. The salary is approximately $9 to $12 an hour.

To find out more information, call "Marketing Research" groups listed in the yellow pages or the phone numbers listed above under "Focus Groups."

Good luck.

- **BENEFITS:** Steady income; flexible shifts.
- **PITFALLS:** Cold calling.
- **SOURCES:** Yellow pages under "Market Research."
- **NEEDS:** Good phone manner.

Messenger

A messenger picks up letters, documents, contracts, checks, or packages and delivers them from one business or individual to another. Most messenger services require you to have a car, driver's license, registration, liability insurance, and working knowledge of the city (or a good map). In New York City a car is not required; in fact most deliveries there are made by foot or by bike. A positive attitude, physical fitness, and a presentable appearance are what most companies look for when hiring.

Many messenger services are open twenty-four hours a day, seven days a week, so a variety of shifts are available. You have the freedom of working alone while making your delivery, and when driving, you can pack your car with plenty of music or books on tape. Foot and bike messengers get plenty of exercise. On the negative side, this job can be stressful if you are facing a deadline and find yourself stuck in traffic (very common in large cities).

Most messengers work on commission. Typically, services pay 50 percent of the particular job or $6 to $8 an hour, plus commission. Overall, you can expect to earn $8 to $15 an hour. Since messengers are usually paid by the delivery, the faster you are, the more money you make. But remember to drive carefully!

Messenger services are always looking for reliable workers. Check the yellow pages under "Messenger Service" for a complete listing or the classifieds under "Messengers" or "Drivers."

Good luck.

- **BENEFITS:** Varied shifts; sense of freedom in car or on bike; decent salary.
- **PITFALLS:** Traffic, irregular income when working on commission; dangerous work, especially for New York bike messengers.
- **SOURCES:** Yellow pages under "Messenger Service." Classifieds under "Messengers" and "Drivers."
- **NEEDS:** Car or bike; knowledge of your city; driver's license, registration, insurance.

Real Estate Agent

Interacting well with people, enjoying the art of selling, patience, and tenacity are some of the qualities needed for success in the world of real estate. Selling real estate on a part-time basis allows you to juggle your hours to suit your needs. There are different facets to being a real estate agent: A buyer's agent represents the buyer solely; a seller's agent (also called a listing agent) represents the seller. A transaction broker has no fiduciary ("loyalty") to either party involved. He or she simply facilitates the transaction. A dual agent represents the buyer and seller simultaneously in showing a broker's (employer's) listing. Note that each state has its own governing rules regarding agency. To become a real estate agent, a college degree is not necessary, but you will need to pass the state exam and in most cities own a car.

Typically, a principal real estate course has to be taken. You can contact real estate brokerage firms and local colleges for desirable class information, or contact specific real estate schools listed in the yellow pages. Expect to pay several hundred dollars for a real estate license and the course, depending on the state you live in. In many states, once you pass your state exam, solicit brokerage firms for employment. Another way to procure employment is to call firms that advertise in the Sunday paper's real estate section. Hanging your license with a broker will provide you with advertising, a desk, a phone, a fax, a copier, information, and voice mail.

Once you are a certified real estate agent, your broker will provide you with MLS (multiple listing service) listings, which is a computer printout of houses or apartments for sale in specified areas. Another way to find houses or apartments to represent is to look for "fisbos" (for sale by owner) in the real estate classified sections. Yet another method is to persuade listings that have expired in the MLS to renew with you!

Most successful part-time real estate agents partner with established agents in their brokers' offices when getting started, working at a lesser commission. You will often need to do most of the grunt work, which entails detailed paperwork, phone solicitations, and taking out new buyers. On the upside, you will gain experience and have access to higher-quality listings while building a reputation. A few common ways to sell properties include advertising on the Internet, through newspapers, on local cable stations, and in the specialized real estate magazines often found at supermarkets and gas stations.

Earnings vary tremendously. It helps if you don't have to worry about your income for the first three to six months since it takes a while to get the ball rolling (closings generally occur after sixty to ninety days), and being desperate when selling is a serious faux pas. Some part-timers make as much as $30,000 to $60,000 a year. Expect to earn 3 to 6 percent of each sale when listing and selling the property. You'll earn at least 1.5 percent when the commission is split between two brokers (listing and selling sides).

Good luck.

- **BENEFITS:** Constantly changing pace and environment; meeting new people; flexible hours; weekend work.
- **PITFALLS:** Fluctuating income; up-front costs; advertising expenses.
- **SOURCES:** Board or association of realtors in your city or state. Contact brokerage firms in your area for information. Check the yellow pages under "Real Estate" and "Schools."
- **NEEDS:** Real estate license, reliable car, sales ability, personality, and perseverance.

Real Estate Appraiser

Appraisers are hired by mortgage brokers, lenders, and banks to appraise a piece of property for current market value. Appraisal is the unscientific art of evaluating a property on the basis of knowledge and information obtained from comparable properties, typically within a mile or two radius or within a subdivision. Banks and mortgage lenders want appraisals on anything that they lend money for. The appraisal plays an important role in whether the lender will lend money to the buyer.

Real estate agents often do appraisals on the side to make extra money. Work is flexible since you often have two to three days to get any given job done. Typically, half the work is done in the field, and half in research. It takes approximately one hour to complete the computer work and visit the property. Using a camera and an MLS (multiple listing service) program, you can give a quick appraisal by knowing location prices, square footage, and number of rooms.

To become a real estate appraiser, you must go to appraisal school and pass a state exam. To get started, contact local real estate offices, the board or association of realtors, and adult ed schools for class information. After you have met your state requirements, contact major banks, lenders, brokers, and appraisal companies for employment opportunities.

Wages vary. Expect to earn about $50,000 per year as an appraiser in major cities.

Note: Another option pertaining to real estate is to work as a photographer for the MLS. Shooting pictures of properties does not require an appraiser license and usually pays $8 to $15 an hour.

Good luck.

- **BENEFITS:** Flexibility; being able to do a number of appraisals in a day.

- **PITFALLS:** Tedious research.
- **SOURCES:** Appraisal school. Local real estate offices. The board or association of realtors. Adult ed schools. Hooking up with real estate agents or appraisal companies.
- **NEEDS:** Car; camera; real estate appraiser license.

Restaurant Work

Although "waitressing on the side" has become something of a cliché, restaurant work continues to be a popular job because it provides fast cash and free or discounted meals. Hours vary, it's a social atmosphere, and there are usually plenty of people on the staff with whom you can trade shifts.

When looking for a restaurant job, be in tune with your own particular needs and criteria. If you are not a night owl, look for a family-style restaurant or at least one that closes by midnight. Also, pay attention to the surrounding environment. I am a nonsmoking, nondrinking morning person who prefers quiet environments (sounds like a personal ad), but at times I worked in smoke-filled pubs and smoke-filled cafés. These were by far my shortest restaurant experiences. Get the point?

BARTENDER

A bartender's duties include setting up the bar, stocking beverages, maintaining an inventory of items, cutting fruit for the condiment tray, cleaning glassware, and mixing drinks for bar customers and the wait staff. Unfortunately, good bartending jobs are not easy to come by since they are often filled from within or through recommendations. Gaining your employer's trust is a key factor in securing a bartending position because you are responsible for the cash register. Generally, you deal directly with the owners, not managers. Bartenders tend to be treated with more respect than waiters because customers want that extra shot of alcohol in their drink.

As with most restaurant jobs, the hours are flexible. You can work day or evening shifts and switch with other bartenders as needed. Day shifts are usually slower and more peaceful, but you earn less money than at night. However, day shifts can be very profitable in business districts such as New York's Wall Street. Salary varies widely, depending on the restaurant, hours, location, and customers. Shift pay is generally $50 to $75 plus tips. Tips are often high because they include gratuities from bar customers as well as a percentage of the wait staff's take. You can expect to earn an average of $80 a day and $125 a night.

If you are presently lacking in bartending experience and knowledge of mixed drinks, plenty of reputable bartending courses are available. Schools usually charge between $300 and $500 for a course, with scholarships and creative financing often available. Many schools will help place you in jobs upon completion. A few reputable ones are the National Bartenders School, American Bartenders School, and Professional Bartending School of New England. Two popular books on mixology are *Mr. Boston's Official Bartending Guide*, published by Warner Books, and *The Original Guide to American Cocktails and Drinks*, published by Bar Media.

Good luck.

- **BENEFITS:** Quick cash, free meals.
- **PITFALLS:** Competitive position; having to be on your feet for an entire shift; dealing with rowdy drunks.
- **SOURCES:** Classifieds. Word of mouth. *Mr. Boston's Official Bartending Guide*, published by Warner Books, *The Original Guide to American Cocktails and Drinks* published by Bar Media. Placement service of bartending schools: National Bartenders School, 800-646-MIXX, www.national bartenders.com; American Bartenders School, 800-736-1001, www.barbook.com; New England Bartending Schools, 781-646-9900, from outside New England, 888-437-

4657, www.bartendingschool.com/NewEngland. American Bartenders' Association, 800-935-3232, www.american bartenders.org.

- **NEEDS:** Wide knowledge of mixology; experience.

HOST/MAÎTRE D'

Hosting involves taking reservations, answering the phone, and greeting and seating people who enter the restaurant. Owners prefer hiring a person who is attractive, neat in appearance, and personable. Your choice of wardrobe will depend on the style of restaurant in which you work. Unfortunately, this job requires that you be on your feet for your entire shift, and when business is slow, the job can be dull. On a positive note, you meet a lot of people, and the job provides flexibility. Different shifts are available, and it's usually possible to switch with another host or maître d'.

Hours vary. Some restaurants prefer you to be there before they open to take reservations. Other locations may require you to work only during the busier hours. Choose a place that you are interested in, and present yourself during off-hours (3:00 P.M. to 5:00 P.M. and 9:00 A.M. to 11:00 A.M.). The best way to get a host or hostess or maître d' position is through a friend's recommendation.

Pay ranges from $7 to $15 an hour, and often you are "tipped out" a small percentage by the wait staff. You may also be tipped by guests who want good tables.

Good luck.

- **BENEFITS:** Easy work; meeting people; discounted or free meals.
- **PITFALLS:** Always being on your feet; boredom at times.
- **SOURCES:** Choose restaurants you are interested in, and present yourself during off-hours (3:00 P.M. to 5:00 P.M. and 9:00 A.M. to 11:00 A.M.).

- **NEEDS:** Neat and presentable appearance; courteous manner.

MANAGER

A manager's duties vary according to restaurant size. They typically include scheduling and monitoring staff efficiency, hiring, firing, bookkeeping, and ordering. The manager serves as a liaison among the floor staff, kitchen staff, and owners and works to ensure customer satisfaction, which often requires table visits. At the end of the day a manager closes out by balancing the cash and charges with the computer or register receipts. Computer knowledge is often necessary.

Managing a restaurant offers a steady salary and is a high-profile, respected job. Management tends to be the least flexible restaurant position since exchanging shifts is limited to the number of managers working in the specific establishment. Prior food service management or headwaiter experience is required, but you can always work up the ranks from within.

Salary varies, depending on restaurant size and type. You can expect to make anywhere from $500 to a $1,000 a week and up. To find a management position, check the classifieds or contact employment agencies through the yellow pages. Word of mouth and a recommendation are best.

Good luck.

- **BENEFITS:** Steady salary; respected position; free meals.
- **PITFALLS:** A lot of responsibility; limited flexibility; long hours; few days off.
- **SOURCES:** Classifieds; word of mouth; employment agencies.
- **NEEDS:** Restaurant experience; computer proficiency.

WAITER/WAITRESS

A waiter's job is to take food and drink orders, serve the requested items, and tend to customer needs. Side work involves setting up tables, refilling condiments, polishing glasses and silver, and cleaning counters and work areas. It is important to be efficient and personable. Having a good memory is definitely an asset since you will need to know and recite the daily specials. Sometimes a more extensive knowledge of wine and food is required.

The positive aspects of being a waiter are fast cash, a flexible schedule, and free meals. The hours vary, depending on the restaurant and your shift assignment. On the downside, you'll have to work at a frantic pace during peak hours and put up with sometimes erratic income; poor tips can alter your mood pretty darn fast.

Salary consists of minimum wage plus tips. Tips will vary, depending on the location and size of the restaurant. An average dinner shift in a mid-size restaurant in a major city pays $80 to $120 a night, and an average lunch shift pays $40 to $80.

When looking for a job, be aware that not all restaurants do well. Before accepting, or even applying, try to gauge the volume of customers as well as the prices on the menu; tips are commensurate with these factors. To get started, look in the help wanted section of the newspaper, ask friends, or apply at restaurants during off-hours (3:00 P.M. to 5:00 P.M. and 9:00 A.M. to 11:00 A.M.).

Good luck.

- **BENEFITS:** Fast cash; flexible hours; free or discounted meals.
- **PITFALLS:** Unsteady income; need to be on your feet; rude customers.

- **SOURCES:** Classifieds. Friends. Visiting restaurants during off-peak hours.
- **NEEDS:** Prior experience and contacts are beneficial but not necessary.

Secret Shopper

Would you believe that someone will actually pay you to shop? For years, retailers have hired secret shoppers, also called mystery shoppers, to check up on the service and attitude of employees and evaluate store operations by posing as customers. This helps store, restaurant, and shopping center owners keep an eye on their staffs and consequently improves customer service. It allows you to earn money while unleashing your wildest consumer fantasies.

Companies that hire secret shoppers look for people who blend in with the crowd. Retail or management experience is often preferred. It is often tiring work. You may have to shop at ten different stores within a three-hour period, and you are required to fill out detailed evaluation forms. On the upside, the wages are good, there is no dress code, and you can shop for yourself while on the job. The hours are flexible—usually fifteen to twenty hours per week—but the amount of available work may vary, depending on where you live.

The pay is about $10 to $15 for evaluation of a store, which can take anywhere from ten minutes to an hour. If you are evaluating a restaurant, a free meal is included. A couple of national companies to contact for information are Feedback Plus and Courtesy Counts. Many of such companies run ads in college newspapers, so check those for employment opportunities. Another idea is to contact large department stores, hotels, or major apartment management firms and ask them which companies they use for this purpose. Some market research companies also hire secret shoppers, so check the yellow pages under "Market Research."

Good luck.

- **BENEFITS:** Flexible schedule; no dress code; being paid to shop.
- **PITFALLS:** Detailed work; weariness (shopping at ten stores in one day can be exhausting—unless you're Ivana Trump).
- **SOURCES:** College newspapers. Contacting major stores or hotels and national companies. Check yellow pages under "Market Research" and the "Market Research" section of this chapter. Feedback Plus, 800-882-SHOP, www.feed backplusinc.com; Courtesy Counts, 800-233-7751, www. courtesycounts.com.
- **NEEDS:** Retail experience preferred.

Sitting Open Houses

Real estate agencies often hire people to sit at tables during open houses and hand out material on the houses or apartments for sale so that the agents can spend more time hustling sales or commissions. When I was in college, my roommate sat open houses on the weekends. It was an excellent part-time job because she was able to study and write in between handing out information. Some apartment managers and owners also hire people to hand out lease applications.

In certain states, such as Florida, you need to be licensed as a real estate agent to hand out information and show people listings, unless you're working for a developer. But in most cases, like that of my roommate, all you need is a professional and responsible manner. It is important to be reliable, punctual, and above all friendly since you will be meeting quite a lot of people and will be acting as a representative of the agency you work for.

Weekend work is plentiful, and even in states where a license is needed, you can always work during the week on brokers' day, when brokers check out new listings. You don't need to be licensed to work a brokers' day.

Wages vary, but you can expect to earn $8 to $12 an hour in major cities. You are usually required to work a minimum of three hours. Shifts can be available all day, depending on when the property is being shown. If you are a licensed real estate agent, you can often choose to forgo an hourly wage in exchange for a percentage of the sale. To get this type of job, all you need to do is let real estate agents know you're available. One idea might be to design a flyer and drop it off with real estate agencies in your area. Read the real estate section of your newspaper, and pick out the heavy hitters to contact; they all have many houses or apartments to show and can probably use your help.

Good luck.

- **BENEFITS:** Flexible hours; catching up on reading or correspondence while sitting.
- **PITFALLS:** Tedium if you don't enjoy being alone.
- **SOURCES:** Real estate agents or companies.
- **NEEDS:** Professional appearance and attitude; reliability and punctuality; enjoyment of working with people.

Supermarket Cashier

A supermarket cashier, also known as a checker (market lingo), rings up the customer's groceries and is responsible for collecting the correct amount of money. It's a great part-time job, and the hours and shifts are flexible since many of today's supermarkets are open twenty-four hours. Some even prefer you to work weekends, ideal for anyone who has a job during the week.

One advantage of this job is knowing when there are sales, which can enable you to save hundreds of dollars on your grocery bill. You also receive full union benefits at major supermarket chains after three months of employment. On the downside, it can be difficult to get a job as a checker if you are just starting out. You may have to invest a few months of low-paying work, about $6 to $7 an hour, as a grocery bagger (wrapper), in order to be promoted from within.

Cashier pay starts around $7 to $9 at most supermarkets, but at many union supermarkets the pay range is $9 to $15 an hour. To get a job, simply visit the stores of your choice, and ask to fill out an application.

Good luck.

- **BENEFITS:** Union support; medical coverage; flexible hours.
- **PITFALLS:** Dealing with a major corporation; needing to be promoted from within.
- **SOURCES:** Go to supermarkets at desired locations and apply.
- **NEEDS:** Friendliness; some cashier experience or an investment of time doing low-paying work.

Telemarketing

Telemarketing involves phone solicitation for a particular product or service. A corporation or an individual will hire you either to cold call (call a list of people who have not yet expressed an interest in your product) or to contact individuals who may have expressed an interest but have not yet purchased the product or service. Most companies provide you with lists of specific people who are in a particular market, sect, or niche that may be interested in what you are selling. The product you market can vary tremendously, from office and computer supplies to season theater tickets to dating services. This is a great job for someone who is articulate, has a positive attitude, enjoys the art of selling (it is best to think of it as introducing an important and beneficial service)—and can handle rejection.

Telemarketing offers flexibility at a decent and sometimes excellent wage. Shifts vary, but they usually last four to six hours. A morning shift typically ends by 1:00 P.M., and afternoon and evening shifts are available for late risers. On the downside, you may have to deal with people being rude to you (but at least you can hang up, unless they beat you to it!) and hearing a lot of "not interested," which can be frustrating. If you are working on commission, "not interested" can mean "no rent money" this month.

There are many telemarketing opportunities out there. It is important to trust the product or service you are selling so that you can put your own enthusiasm into your marketing pitch. It often helps when the company you work for offers potential customers a trial or gift certificate over the phone; everyone likes a freebie.

For specific telemarketing jobs, check the classifieds under "Telemarketing," "Sales," and "Part-time Work." Trade papers and college newspapers often list telemarketing jobs as well. Find one that best suits your needs in terms of service, geographic location, salary, and commission. Income varies widely among telemarketing jobs, usually ranging from $7 to $20 an hour. Salary plus commission is the norm; others are commission only. The latter can pay extremely well if it's a high-end product or service; some employees earn over $50,000 a year for a thirty-hour workweek.

Good luck.

- **BENEFITS:** Flexible shifts; good salary; often health benefits.
- **PITFALLS:** Needing to deal with rejection; feeling isolated if you're working in a cubicle.
- **SOURCES:** Classified section under "Telemarketing," "Sales," and "Part-time." Trade papers. College newspapers.
- **NEEDS:** Positive attitude; upbeat personality; knowledge of your product or service; persistence; good communication skills.

Valet Parking

You can work at the finest establishments, meet famous people, and stand face-to-face with the heads of studios. Valet parking is a job that offers glamour and earns a substantial wage. Flexible shifts are available around the clock. The qualifications include having a driver's license, a clean driving record, a Social Security card, and, as one company put it, the ability to "smile and say hello."

Pay varies. Typically it is minimum wage plus tips, but it may be as much as $8 an hour plus tips. When it's all added up, you can expect to make $9 to $20 an hour. You can usually earn more money at busy upscale restaurants or hotels than at private parties.

For employment, check local newspapers and magazines or the yellow pages under "Parking Attendant Service" and "Valet Service." Call hotels or restaurants in your area to find out what valet companies they use.

Good luck.

- **BENEFITS:** Possibly meeting famous people; driving cool cars (albeit for short distances); flexible shifts; steady work.

- **PITFALLS:** You have to give the keys back.
- **SOURCES:** Local newspapers and magazines. Yellow pages under "Parking Attendant Service" and "Valet Service."
- **NEEDS:** Energetic and friendly personality; driver's license; clean driving record; Social Security card.

Video Store Clerk

"Play it again, Sam," or in this case, rent it again. Everybody loves the convenience, the price, the selection, and the chance to pop popcorn and curl up in front of an old favorite. Each video store needs a number of helpful clerks, and that's where you come in: You look up movies for customers and check out rentals.

Working in a video store is a great part-time job for anyone interested in the film industry. Since you are constantly doing research, you will learn a lot about genres of film and who the different directors and lead actors are. In large cities, many video stores are open until midnight, allowing for flexibility in scheduling shifts. Knowledge of a wide variety of films is preferred but not necessary.

Starting salary is normally $7 to $9 an hour, and most stores offer the bonus of free rentals and discounts on merchandise. There are many video stores to choose from. Look in your yellow pages under "Video Tapes" and "Discs—Renting and Leasing," and frequent the stores you are interested in. Find out when the manager is in and set up an interview. Many people have told me that Tower Records and Video is a particularly good place to work because it provides health coverage.

Good luck.

- **BENEFITS:** Flexible scheduling; learning about films; free rentals and discounts.

- **PITFALLS:** Low starting salary.
- **SOURCES:** Neighborhood stores. Yellow pages under "Video Tapes" and "Discs—Renting and Leasing."
- **NEEDS:** Good attitude; social skills; film knowledge preferred.

3

That's Entertainment

THERE'S NO BUSINESS
LIKE SHOW BUSINESS

Box Office Salesperson

These days it seems as if you have to take out a second mortgage on your house to afford a night out at the theater. Theater tickets are expensive, but there is a way to see all the latest shows without going into debt: work part-time as a box office salesperson. Working the box office for a theater company or performing arts center will allow you to indulge your taste for the dramatic arts without spending enormous amounts of money.

Basically three jobs are involved in this line of work. One is to work directly in the box office assisting customers who step up to the window to purchase tickets. A second way is to work for a company in your area that handles ticket sales for many theaters and performing arts centers, such as Ticketmaster. Such a company will hire people to work the box office over the phone. A third way is to work in a theater or performing arts center answering phones and providing details on the show, show times, and other information. Some theaters will employ you simply to answer phones, while others will have you answer questions as well as sell tickets.

There are many shifts to choose from when working the box office. Shows are usually "dark" (off for the night, in theater lingo) on Mondays. Some performing arts centers, however, are open 365 days a year. Holidays in particular are big business; there is even work to be had on Christmas (remember *The Nutcracker*). To find employment, contact theaters and performing arts centers listed in your paper's entertainment section. Also look in the yellow pages under "Theaters." Pay varies, depending on experience and the venue you work. Working the box office at a theater where you personally meet people usually pays more. Pay is typically $7 to $12 an hour.

Good luck.

- **BENEFITS:** Seeing shows (usually from orchestra seats) for free or at a discount; steady hourly wage.
- **PITFALLS:** Dealing with people who are upset with policies or cancellation of shows in their subscription.
- **SOURCES:** Contacting theaters and performing arts centers.
- **NEEDS:** Professionalism; ability to cope with people and their requests or problems.

Choir Work

Did you know that it's possible to get paid for singing beautiful hymns and prayers? In most major cities, temples and churches hire singers and musicians for their choirs. Even if you have no formal voice training, most organists and choir directors, who are always on the lookout for new talent, will listen to new singers if they have proficient sight-reading skills.

Church and temple choir members typically earn anywhere from $50 to $100 a service. This fee may include a two-hour rehearsal one weekday evening and another rehearsal right before the service on Saturday or Sunday morning. Salary may vary, depending on specific skills.

Music schools, such as Juilliard and the Manhattan School of Music, post choir opportunities on their student service bulletin boards. Most self-respecting organists and choir directors belong to the American Guild of Organists (AGO), headquartered in New York, with local chapters all across the country and a chapter in Canada called the Royal Canadian College of Organists (RCCO). Membership includes a subscription to its magazine, which lists employment opportunities. Another way to procure employment is to look up churches in your phone book and send a résumé to the music directors. Voice teachers and their students are another useful resource.

Good luck.

- **BENEFITS:** Networking; performing; spiritual work; possibility of solos.
- **PITFALLS:** Chorus work if you want to be a soloist.
- **SOURCES:** American Guild of Organists, www.agohq.org, headquarters in New York, 212-870-2310; in Canada, call the Royal Canadian College of Organists, 416-929-6400. Contact musical directors at churches and temples.
- **NEEDS:** Musical abilities; sight-reading skills.

Cruise Ship Entertainer

If you can sing, dance, play an instrument, make people laugh, or do magic tricks, entertaining on a cruise ship can be a great way to make money, perform, and vacation, all at the same time. Cruise ships hire dancers and singers for musical revues, various performers for individual acts, musicians for bands and solo work, and pianists for cocktail lounges. The act hired is specific to the cruise ship. Individual acts can be hired for two days or six months, depending on the contract and the company. You can be booked directly by the cruise line or through an agent.

To be booked directly, you usually need to send a videotape, showcasing your talents, to the entertainment operations department of the specific cruise line you want to work for. Nationwide auditions for musical revue performers and other talent are held once or twice a year. They are advertised in the trade papers (*Backstage West* in Los Angeles and *Backstage* in New York), or you can call the cruise line to find out when auditions will be held.

The advantage of working with a booking agent (10 to 20 percent commission) is the agent's insider knowledge of specific cruise lines and ability to know where your act will fit best. Dancers and singers for revues are typically paid $300 to $500 a week plus room and board. Principal performers in revues can make up to $1,500 a week. Contracts for revues are usually three to six months (a great way to save some money). An individual show (comedian, singer, magician) will run about ten to thirty minutes, and pay starts at about $1,000 a week plus room and board. Your work will probably consist of two shows performed two nights a week, so you're onstage only about two hours each week!

Good luck.

- **BENEFITS:** Getting to perform; paid vacations; travel; social environment; great wages.
- **PITFALLS:** A six-month contract can take you away from friends, family, and your career.
- **SOURCES:** Cruise lines or booking agents. A couple of booking agents are Bramson Entertainment, 630 Ninth Avenue, Suite 203, New York, NY 10036, 212-265-3500. In Florida: 954-423-8853, www.bramson.com; Don Casino

Productions, 20880 West Dixie Hwy., Suite 105, Miami, FL 33180, 305-931-7552, www.doncasino.com. A few popular cruise ship companies to contact directly are Royal Caribbean Cruises Ltd., Entertainment Department, 1050 Port Blvd., Miami, FL 33132, 305-539-6000, www.royal-caribbean.com; Princess Cruises, Fleet Personnel Department, 24844 Avenue Rockefeller, Santa Clarita, CA 91355, 818-376-6767 or 800-PRINCESS, www.princess.com; Royal Olympic Cruises, Entertainment Department, 805 Third Avenue New York, NY 10022, 800-872-6400, www.royalolympiccruises.com; Carnival Cruise Lines, 3655 NW Eighty-seventh Avenue, Miami, FL 33178, 305-599-2600; American Hawaii Cruises, 700 Bishop St., Suite 800, Honolulu, HI 96813, 808-538-8200; Crystal Cruise Line, Entertainment Department, 2049 Century Park E, Suite 1400, Los Angeles, CA 90067, 310-785-9300, www.crystalcruises. com.

- **NEEDS:** Talent; a musical act; enjoyment of cruises and traveling.

Extra Work

"There are no small parts"—or so the saying goes. Imagine the movie *The Ten Commandments* without the twenty thousand extras. Pretty boring! Extras, or background performers, as they are now referred to in this era of politically correct language, are used to give atmosphere to a set and life to scenes in which the principal actors are the focus. For the novice actor, extra work is a terrific way to learn the many facets of the movie and TV industry. You get to see what goes on behind the camera as well as how fellow (albeit more experienced) thespians work. In certain situations, extras are given a line of dialogue, upgraded in pay scale, and asked to join the union.

To become eligible for extra work, go to a casting office that deals with background performers, and drop off a photo. Many agencies have particular days for this, so call ahead for information. Some services charge a nominal fee for nonunion members. A word of warning: Be wary of agencies that charge more than a $30 fee or insist on expensive photos. It is also helpful and more profitable (you get a wardrobe stipend) if you can provide your own wardrobe for the roles you play (uniforms, upscale clothing, costumes).

Wages vary depending on your city. In Los Angeles, nonunion extras make about $60 for eight hours, and Screen Actors Guild (SAG) union extras make $110. In New York, rates start at $115. This hourly rate goes up with overtime.

For a list of reputable casting offices, check the *Ross Reports*, found at theatrical bookstores and major newsstands. Look in your yellow pages under "Casting Services," or call reputable agents and casting directors asking for referral numbers. SAG's production services department has listings of casting directors. *Movie Extra Work for Rocket Scientists*, by Cullen Chambers, provides more information than you probably need, but it's a great book and can be found at most theatrical bookstores.

Good luck.

- **BENEFITS:** Work on a professional TV or movie set; possibility of being upgraded; contacts.
- **PITFALLS:** Long hours.
- **SOURCES:** Contact casting offices that deal with background performers. Production services department of SAG, 213-549-6811. *Movie Extra Work for Rocket Scientists*, by Cullen Chambers. In Los Angeles, call Central Casting (SAG union only), 818-562-2888, ext. 3200; Cenex (for nonunion), 818-562-2888, ext. 3219; Idell James Casting, 310-230-9344. In New York, try Wilfley Grant Casting,

212-685-3537, and Sylvia Fay Casting, 212-889-2626. In Hollywood, Florida, try Famous Faces, 954-922-0700. In Chicago, call K.T.'s, 773-525-1126.

• **NEEDS:** Professional attitude.

Industry Showcase Organizer

Organizing industry showcases for actors, musicians, and singers can be an excellent way to earn money with your creative, organizational, and networking abilities. Showcases have become increasingly popular as a way for hopeful actors to display their talents to important industry members. Agency representatives may sign up performing artists they like, and casting directors or producers may call them in to audition for specific projects. These rewards do happen often. Hence the popularity of showcases and the willingness of performing artists to pay to participate.

Performing as an actor in a showcase is similar to being in a play, albeit an extremely short play. The showcase generally takes place in a recognized theater space, with about eight or ten scenes (usually five to ten minutes each) being performed by about twenty actors. This enables actors to show their best comedic or dramatic prepared material while "talent scouts" watch.

Your job as the showcase organizer is to recruit performing artists, rent theater space, organize a dinner buffet, create the showcase flyers and programs, and advertise the showcase for industry attendance. You can gather singers, musicians, and actors through friends, flyers, acting classes and workshops, advertisements in the trades, or theater companies. First-rate, centrally located theaters will draw the highest industry response.

The first thing to do is to book your space. Performing arts bookstores usually have information on theaters, or you can check the yellow pages under "Theaters." To draw agents, managers, casting people, and producers, you can place advertisements in local papers or deliver individual packets to your targeted market.

Your profit will depend on the overhead costs. Most showcases charge $200 to $400 per person for two to four nights of performing in the arranged showcase. An actress I went to college with puts on showcases every two months. She charges $350 per person, and each then performs a scene four nights (two nights a week, two consecutive weeks). She makes at least a few thousand dollars' profit per showcase, and she often acts in them as well.

Good luck.

- **BENEFITS:** Networking; you can perform in them too!
- **PITFALLS:** Gathering actors, musicians, and singers for each showcase; risk of being thought of as a producer who runs showcases, rather than as a performing artist.
- **SOURCES:** The trades. Networking. Yellow pages.
- **NEEDS:** Business mind; organizational skills; networking ability.

Industry Workshop and Seminar Organizer

Organizing industry workshops and seminars for all kinds of professions is becoming increasingly popular as a way to make money while staying connected to a particular industry. Some examples include a financial service seminar, a computer seminar, an actors' workshop, and a real estate seminar. You can gear your workshop or seminar toward writers, musicians, new parents, or almost any area of interest.

For example, setting up an industry workshop for actors would entail renting a studio and having about ten to twenty actors pay $20 to $40 to meet and do cold readings for a casting director, an agent, or a producer. It may seem unfair that actors should have to pay to meet a casting director, but this type of service often leads to work or signing with an agent. Seminars feature a panel of experts, sometimes over a two-day period, and participants pay a higher fee (usually a few hundred dollars). The profit margin will depend on your overhead (space rental fee, price of flyer reproduction and distribution, and cost of moderator or panel). Good business sense, organization, and promotional skills are necessary for success.

To get started, visit a few similar workshops or seminars, usually advertised in the industry trade papers, and talk to others to learn what works well and what doesn't. Ask friends in the field what kind of workshop they would be interested in attending. You may want to start with very little overhead. You can rent a space at a modest price (check the trade papers) or rent a hotel room and gather people through personal contacts and by placing advertisements in industry trade papers. Someone with experience is hired to lead a particular industry workshop and will need to be paid for his or her time (the going rate starts at about $100), unless you can call in a favor or do some kind of work-related exchange.

Good luck.

- **BENEFITS:** Meeting industry contacts; being a part of the workshops and seminars yourself.
- **PITFALLS:** Tough to gather actors and industry personnel.
- **SOURCES:** The trades. Networking.
- **NEEDS:** Business mind; organizational skills.

Karaoke Performer

Welcome to the Japanese version of the sing-along. Originally imported from Japan, karaoke has become quite the rage in the States. A karaoke machine enables anyone to sing a favorite musical number by deleting the lead vocals and playing only the background and accompaniment. Lyrics are supplied on lead sheets or a video screen.

As a karaoke performer you have to inspire others to break out of their shells and into song. You don't need to be an excellent singer to work a karaoke party. Often if you are too good, you may intimidate wanna-be singers. The quality of singing and level of experience required of a karaoke artist varies from gig to gig, but the objective is always to make people relax and have a good time. The parties are almost always at night, although the hours vary, depending on the club. Shifts usually run from 8:00 P.M. to midnight or 10:00 P.M. to 2:00 A.M.

To get a job with an existing company, check the trade papers (*Backstage*, for example) for karaoke artists. Often the jobs are listed under the guise of a "singer wanted" advertisement. You can also go to any nightclub that has karaoke and look through its karaoke magazine to find ads with phone numbers and possible employment opportunities. Call and ask if they are hiring singers.

If you have an entrepreneurial spirit and some spare cash, you can buy or rent karaoke equipment and start your own business. You will need to advertise your service in clubs, bars, and restaurants. Or you can work private functions. Go to places that do karaoke, check them out, and ask questions.

Even if you love the idea of being your own boss, it may be a good idea to work for an existing karaoke company first to learn the ropes. Check the yellow pages under "Entertainers." When you work as an employee, the pay generally ranges from

$10 to $18 an hour. If it is your own business and you supply the equipment, charge what market value will bear.

Good luck.

- **BENEFITS:** Learning and performing songs; good hourly wage; having fun; meeting people.
- **PITFALLS:** Unsteady income.
- **SOURCES:** Check trade papers. Call karaoke companies. Look at yellow pages under "Entertainers."
- **NEEDS:** Singing ability; outgoing personality.

Location Manager

A location manager is responsible for finding places for photographers or film companies to shoot outside the studio arena, such as a home or commercial space. Your job is to make arrangements to use the space involved, facilitate the "intrusion," and see that everything goes according to plan.

Besides finding locations, you will be involved in securing permits from the city, the state, or the police department—whatever is necessary. Your job will be to negotiate fees with property owners or individual cities and towns and to handle insurance matters. The police and local film board may need to be involved to make sure all rules and regulations are followed.

To work in this field, you should be familiar with the area you're representing, including interiors. Photographers and directors may be looking for anything from a mansion to a 1940s barbershop. To find employment, build a portfolio of pictures of places you know and can get permission to shoot in. Do your research, and then go around to photographers and film companies in the area with your portfolio. Most major cities and all states have a film board to call for information on film companies. You can also call the governor's office to track down numbers; ask for the person who handles film permits, and go from there.

It is always a good idea to apprentice when starting out, but you can make excellent money as a freelancer. Salary varies, depending on the city and work involved, so call local competitors for rates. Expect to earn a few hundred dollars a day.

Good luck.

- **BENEFITS:** Outlet for creativity; good pay; flexible scheduling, depending on when the shoot is.
- **PITFALLS:** Long hours.
- **SOURCES:** Film companies. Photographers. Directors. Your city or state's film board.
- **NEEDS:** Problem-solving ability; inventiveness; people skills; patience.

Magician

Performing magic tricks is a specialized skill requiring practice, acting, storytelling abilities, and coordination. If you possess these skills and have an outgoing nature, you will be well suited for this job.

To learn magic tricks, you can purchase a beginner's instructional video for $30 to $80 at a magician supply store (check the yellow pages under "Magician Supplies"). Joining the Society of American Magicians entitles you to many benefits and will enable you to learn the secrets of other magicians. It costs about $65 a year to be a member, and even though the magicians are sworn to secrecy, they are eager and willing to swap tricks with fellow members. This is a great way to get the inside scoop on all sorts of showstoppers. Similarly, the International Brotherhood (women too!) of Magicians has chapters all over the world.

There are many places to perform magic for money. Family-style restaurants often hire magicians to entertain at tables while patrons wait for their food. Card and coin tricks and balloon animals are most appropriate for this type of atmosphere. Some restaurants, however, hold more extensive evening shows and hire their magicians out for private parties. Often entertainment companies (listed in the yellow pages under "Entertainment" and "Party Planning") hire magicians as well for corporate affairs, private parties, trade shows, sales meetings, seminars, and industrial shows. Another idea is to do a mass mailing of flyers directly to companies that are always in need of entertainment for private parties and conventions, such as IBM or Whirlpool. Or advertise in community newsletters, local magazines, and parent newspapers (just think of all those kids' parties). Contact cruise lines (see "Cruise Ship Entertainer," this chapter) and hotels.

Typically a restaurant will pay you $50 to $100 for two hours' work or will ask you to work for tips only. The going rate for one hour of close-up magic (private parties) is $250 to $350. A full-scale show can pay in the thousands. The cost of buying magician props and supplies varies from a few dollars for simple tricks to thousands for full-blown illusions and spectacle. You may want to offer to work private parties and functions for free or a minimum salary while perfecting your skills and building your reputation.

Good luck.

- **BENEFITS:** Getting to hone your comedy and improv skills; short hours; having fun; good money.
- **PITFALLS:** Expensive props and tricks; needing a lot of time and effort to learn; having to market your skills; unsteady income.
- **SOURCES:** Magic stores: in New York, Tannen's Magic, 212-

929-4500. Yellow pages under "Entertainers." The Magic Agency Inc., 212-288-9133, and Wizard Productions, 800-400-3836. To find your local chapter of the Society of American Magicians, go to www.magicsam.com. Contact the headquarters of the International Brotherhood of Magicians, 11155 South Towne Sq., St. Louis, MO 63123, 314-845-9200, www.magician.org. Private parties, hotels, cruise lines.

- **NEEDS:** Outgoing personality; hand dexterity; eye-hand coordination; patience.

Party Enhancer

You don't have to be Robin Williams or Rosie O'Donnell to be the life of the party—or, in this case, a professional party enhancer. Take your abundant talents, your creative ideas, dialects you've spent years perfecting, and the characters you create in front of your bathroom mirror, and make money performing at parties! Corporate events, banquets, film openings, birthday parties, charity events, and private functions are a few of the many events that hire party planning companies to supply ready-made entertainment.

Recently my husband's friend, who owns a catering and event company, called me to assist him with hiring entertainers. He was handling the premiere of a major motion picture and needed actors and comedians to impersonate the lead characters in the film during the reception. It was then that it dawned on me how popular party enhancers are. One person I know earns an excellent living (he just bought a house) impersonating Columbo at corporate parties. He has put together a polished and hysterically funny presentation and hires himself out, often bypassing an agency's cut. An actress told me that her job is impersonating Marilyn Monroe at events and parties. What's more, she raved about the job.

Pay varies, depending on whether you work with an agency or hire yourself out. The typical range when working through an agency is $50 to $250 an hour. For employment opportunities, look in the yellow pages under "Party Planning Services" or in the classified sections of local magazines. Make up a catchy promotional flyer and a business card. For continuous employment enroll with a number of agencies. After you have developed your characters, consider doing singing telegrams (see "Singing Telegrams," this chapter), if you can carry a tune.

Good luck.

- **BENEFITS:** Creative work; having fun; good hourly wage; great food.
- **PITFALLS:** Work may be unsteady.
- **SOURCES:** Yellow pages under "Party Planning Services." Classified sections of local magazines. Self-initiated advertising. In Los Angeles, Mulligan Management, 818-752-9474, www.lookalikes.net, and A Plus Entertainment, 818-901-0559. Deco Productions, in Miami, does conventions and high-end entertainment; call 305-558-0800. Enchanted Parties, 631-467-6628, www.enchantedparties.com.
- **NEEDS:** Bravery, improvisational skills, well-developed sense of humor.

Personal Assistant

Running personal errands, making travel arrangements, returning phone calls, organizing dinner parties, shopping, carpooling the kids, and taking a pet to the vet are just a few of the responsibilities of a personal assistant. Many people in high-power positions—from celebrities to business executives—hire people to aid them in a variety of ways. Personal assistants need to be extremely organized, responsible, and decisive. You will be dealing with high-profile, powerful people and doing everything that they don't have time to do. Be warned that there is a ton of responsibility involved, both physically and emotionally. Sometimes you are on call twenty-four hours a day.

Salary varies considerably, depending on experience, negotiations, and the generosity of your employer. Personal assistants typically make anywhere from $400 to $1,500 a week. In some cases, an assistant lives on the property of his or her employer, so room and board are paid for as well. A job as a personal assistant can be elusive, especially when it's for a celebrity. Jonathan Holiff, the president of the Association of Celebrity Personal Assistants (ACPA), estimates that there are more than five thousand personal assistants in Hollywood. Most celebrities and powerful people seek referrals, so if you know anyone who has personal relations with celebrities, let him or her know that you are interested in the job. You can also contact employment agencies listed in the yellow pages and look for ads in the trade papers, as well as in the classifieds of your local paper.

The aforementioned Association of Celebrity Personal Assistants is a nonprofit membership-based organization that can help you tremendously in your job search. The membership fee of $100 a year includes access to a job bank for experienced personal assistants between positions. With over 350 members, the organization will assist you in networking with other celebrity assistants and gathering valuable information. ACPA members even teach a course on becoming a personal assistant at the Learning Annex.

Note: In Los Angeles, the Job Factory, an employment service, helps job seekers find flexible employment and receives many personal assistant positions. Membership includes a free résumé service and guaranteed work.

Good luck.

- **BENEFITS:** Travel; invitations to benefits and screenings; exposure to the celebrity world; chance to make contacts.
- **PITFALLS:** Bearing a lot of responsibility; physically and emotionally draining; often hellish hours; catering to the whims of the rich and famous.
- **SOURCES:** Contacts. Advertisements. Association of Celebrity Personal Assistants, 310-281-7755 in Los Angeles and 212-803-5444 in New York, www.celebrityassistants. org. Celebrity Personal Assistants, Inc. in Atlanta, 404-942-5728, www.celebritypersonalassistants. com. The Learning Annex, www.learningannex.com, or call 310-478-6677 in Los Angeles or 212-371-0280 in New York.
- **NEEDS:** Good organizational skills; excellent grooming; responsibility, flexibility; good interpersonal skills.

Pianist for Sketch Comedy and Improv Groups

If you play piano by ear, have a wide range of songs in your repertoire, are a quick thinker, and enjoy working with actors, then somewhere a sketch comedy group wants you. In most major cities there are sketch comedy and improv shows almost every night from about seven to ten-thirty. Working as a pianist is a flexible gig in that you can turn down shows anytime you are unable to attend, as long as you give enough advance notice. The group will tell you exactly what to play or what genre of music it wants to hear during the acts and blackouts and at other times. The job is a lot of fun and a great way to meet people. Best of all, you get to see theater for free. Also, drinks are usually included (as long as you can keep playing). A show generally runs for one to two hours, and the pay averages $50 to $100 per show. Some musicians agree to split the house (the cover charge minus costs) with the cast instead of receiving specific wages.

For employment opportunities, contact improv or sketch comedy groups in your area, and request that your name be put on a list for available piano players. You'll find that the larger market is in sketch comedy simply because there are more of those groups around. Advertise your skills by posting signs at theaters and contacting groups through ads you see in the trades (such as *Backstage*). Consider contacting cocktail lounges (look in the yellow pages under "Cocktail Lounges") for piano bar work as well. As always, the best way to get work is by word of mouth.

Good luck.

- **BENEFITS:** Creative environment; meeting people; using your musical ability.
- **PITFALLS:** Challenge of finding a stable, well-paying group to work with.
- **SOURCES:** Word of mouth. Advertise in the trades. Post signs at theaters. See sketch comedies and schmooze. Call improv groups. A couple of popular groups in Los Angeles are the Groundlings, 323-934-4747, www.groundlings.com; Los Angeles Theatresports, 323-401-6162, www.theatresports.com; and ACME Comedy Theater, 323-525-0233. In New York, try Chicago City Limits, 212-888-5233, www.chicagocitylimits.com, and Gotham City Improv, 212-367-8222, www.gothamcityimprov.com. Call Second City in Chicago at 312-337-3992 or 877-778-4707; in Detroit, 313-965-2222; or to find the location closest to you, visit the Web site www.secondcity.com. In Seattle, call Unexpected Productions, 206-587-2414, www.unexpectedproductions.org.
- **NEEDS:** Enjoyment of working with actors; playing piano well by ear; having a wide repertoire.

Script Reader

If you like to read, have a talent for writing, own a computer or typewriter, and prefer to supplement your income in the leisure of your own home, script reading may be just right for you. Film studios, producers, and literary agents are constantly hiring people to read scripts and then write evaluations, called coverage. This job is especially good for screenwriters who want to sharpen their own critical sensibilities. Flexibility is the most significant advantage of a script-reading position. With some experience, you can even work your way up into a development position. Many major film executives started out as script readers.

There are a number of ways to learn how to become a freelance script reader, especially in major entertainment cities like Los Angeles or New York, where jobs are plentiful. You can take a class in story analysis at adult ed and extension schools, such as UCLA Extension and the Learning Annex, which is now expanding to most major cities. To gain experience and build your résumé, try interning at a reputable theater or film company in your area that accepts and reviews unsolicited materials. Once you have gotten a feel for the basics, contact anyone and everyone you know in the industry. Supplement your personal contacts with *The Hollywood Creative Directory, The Illinois Production Guide,* or *The New York Production Guide (NYPG).* These books, which are available in most theatrical bookstores, list every production company in town. Call small production companies directly; they will probably be easier to break into and may not require much prior experience. You can offer to do a trial coverage to show off your abilities, and then you'll have a sample to pass around. Script readers usually earn $40 to $60 per script. Reading and covering a script generally take three to four hours.

Good luck.

- **BENEFITS:** Working at home; making industry contacts; sharpening critical sensibilities; improving writing skills.
- **PITFALLS:** Tedious work; an overwhelming wealth of poorly written scripts.
- **SOURCES:** Take a class. Call production companies and showbiz contacts. *The Hollywood Creative Directory*, www.hcdonline.com; *The Illinois Production Guide*, 312-814-3600, www.illinoisbiz.biz/film; or *The New York Production Guide (NYPG)*, www.nypg.com. UCLA Extension, 310-825-9971. The Learning Annex: Los Angeles, 310-478-6677; San Francisco, 415-788-5500; San Diego, 619-544-9700; New York, 212-371-0280; for other cities and more information, visit www.learningannex.com.
- **NEEDS:** Enjoyment of reading; writing well; sample coverage of a script.

Singing Telegrams

For all you future "Broadway babies" (and former ones as well), delivering singing telegrams can be a fun way to make money. The only prerequisites are a decent singing voice and minimal dance ability. Most important, you'd better not embarrass easily. Some companies prefer writers, since they think up innovative and quirky telegrams. Anything goes as long as you can carry a tune.

Most telegram deliverers wear tuxedoes or are disguised as gorillas, nerds, bag ladies, or French troubadours. The companies usually supply costumes (or pay you extra if you supply your own), except for the tuxedo, which you are expected to have. Women will need the female version of the messenger tuxedo: fishnet stockings, black heels, a short black skirt or shorts, and a jacket.

The work is flexible, but unsteady, so sign up with a few companies if you want to stay busy. Business booms around Valentine's Day and other holidays, so stay in town and be available to work at these times. Pay is approximately $40 to $60 per telegram. Some companies pay extra for travel time. The routine takes approximately two to fifteen minutes.

To find a job, simply contact singing telegram companies in your area. Companies are listed in the yellow pages under "Entertainers" as well as in local magazines in the advertisement sections. Some may prefer that you have your own costume, but most will help you out with initial material.

Good luck.

- **BENEFITS:** Extremely short shifts; good wages; way to have fun; creative challenges; getting to perform.
- **PITFALLS:** Unsteady employment; minor travel involved.
- **SOURCES:** Yellow pages under "Entertainers." Singing Telegrams Nationwide, 800-545-3354, www.fantasies. qpg.com. In the Los Angeles area, contact Zebra Entertainment, 818-906-3809, www.zebraentertainment.com. In New York, a few good ones are Preppy Grams, 800-936-SING, www.preppygrams.com; Life of the Party, 800-966-7456; and AAA Entertainment, 800-43PARTY, www.1800 PARTY.com.
- **NEEDS:** Upbeat personality; singing and dancing abilities.

Street Performer

If you have any kind of performing ability, you can hit the streets and make quick cash. From musicians and dancers to sketch artists and comedians, people making money off their talents can be found on the curb or in the subways. Wherever there are large crowds of people, you can profit. All you need is a canister or hat to hold the tips—preferably a very large one (think positive!).

There are all kinds of success stories about street performers' being "discovered." Tracy Chapman was "discovered" singing in a subway station, and I know of a musician who got a record contract from performing on the Santa Monica Pier for a number of years. A friend found his wedding entertainment by recruiting a group he saw performing at a street fair.

Anywhere there is heavy pedestrian traffic, such as tourist spots and recreational areas of your city, is a great place to entertain. If you are playing an instrument, you will need to find a good acoustic area or bring along a small amplifier and microphone. In most cities, street performers are required to have a license (a vendor's permit, sometimes referred to as a peddler's license); call your city or county clerk's office for information.

Your income will vary widely, depending on your act, the location, the weather, and how many people gather round. It is possible to earn $50 to $100 for a few hours of performing. You can also earn extra money if you sell tapes of your music. During the holidays people are usually in the giving spirit and enjoy being entertained, so take your act outside and reap the benefits!

Good luck.

- **BENEFITS:** Cash earnings; working outdoors; self-employment.
- **PITFALLS:** Unsteady income; variable weather conditions; distracting city noise.
- **SOURCES:** Popular outdoor spots. Local city or county clerk's office for licensing information.
- **NEEDS:** Chutzpah; amp and microphone for musicians and vocalists; street vendor's license.

Theme Park Performer

Believe it or not, somewhere in the world, Groucho Marx, Charlie Chaplin, and Laurel and Hardy are still performing! In fact, theme parks often hire performers to impersonate a variety of famous comedians and TV personalities, perform in rock and roll shows, sing in musical theater, and risk their lives in stunt shows. This is a great job for actors and singers or anyone who enjoys being center stage. Millions of people visit theme parks every year, so an audience is guaranteed. You get to network with other performers, display your talents, and hone your performance skills. Typically, the job requires improvisational or musical theater skills, but stunt shows may need acrobats, gymnasts, dancers, and stunt people. Even comedians, announcers, magicians, and star impersonators can find work here.

Hours vary, depending on your job and the theme park you are working for. Shifts are usually six to eight hours. A principal performer does multiple shows in a day, with each show lasting twenty to thirty minutes. Extra hours and shifts are available during Christmas, the summer, and spring break. Shifts are flexible because you can usually find a substitute to cover for you.

To attract high-caliber performers, Universal Studios allows its employees to take time off for auditions and interviews as long as all shifts are covered. To make this possible, it hires full-time workers as well as fills on call positions to cover the regulars when needed. It also supports your career aspirations by allowing industry people to attend your performances for free. Many performers have gotten jobs or agents through their work at Universal. If you are a full-time employee, health benefits are available. At Universal, you are paid per show (stint pay), and there are three to four shows in a day. Pay ranges from $22 to $55 a show, depending on experience and what the entertainment department determines. Most shows run twenty minutes, but you're contracted for the full day. If you are a full-time employee (three to four days a week), you are eligible for health benefits.

At Disneyland and Disney World three regular principals are usually hired for each job, along with a few subs. Principal performers must join the union, the American Guild of Variety Artists (AGVA), and are paid about $150 per day plus benefits. Chorus members make about $125 a day plus benefits. Performers are hired to work in the parades, wear character heads, and entertain people in line, but their salaries are much less, starting around $7 to $8 an hour. However, these jobs can be a good way to get in with the company, and regular pay increases are common. Be aware that the work can be extremely demanding (*demanding* is a nice word for *exhausting*). Some shows are held outdoors, and wearing a full-body costume in summer is not always comfortable.

To get these jobs, you will need to audition. Advertisements are listed in the trade papers (*Backstage, Hollywood Reporter,* and *Variety*) in the spring and fall. For information on current auditions for any major theme park, contact the entertainment department.

Good luck.

- **BENEFITS:** Using your talents to perform; making industry contacts.
- **PITFALLS:** Uncomfortable costumes; low hourly wage in some positions.
- **SOURCES:** Hollywood AGVA office, 818-508-9984. Trade papers for audition information. For Universal Studios, call the entertainment department, 818-622-3851. For Walt Disney World auditions, call Talent Casting, 407-397-3299, and for Disneyland, 714-781-0111. For Knotts Berry Farm auditions, call 714-220-5386 or 714-995-6688. Six Flags Magic Mountain, www.sixflags.com.

- **NEEDS:** Training in musical theater; stunt or impersonator skills.

Varied Musical Work

My husband and I are a perfect example of how simple it can be to use your various musical talents to make some extra money. A number of years back, we decided that it would be fun to volunteer our talents by performing at a local Jewish senior center. We both sing and play guitar. Our first gig was rough around the edges, but soon we were taking requests and expanding our repertoire to include show tunes as well as Hebrew and Yiddish songs. Word spread, and soon we were in hot demand, earning $200 to $500 for a thirty- to sixty-minute singing gig. We still enjoy volunteering, but it sure is nice to be paid. Besides performing at many senior centers, retirement homes, and temples, we have sung at nonprofit organizations such as ORT, the City of Hope, veterans associations, sisterhoods, and private parties. If you love to perform, this can be a fantastic way to bring music to appreciative people and to earn good money for a short amount of time.

If you are a singer who plays guitar or piano, you can often hire yourself out as a solo performer and keep all your earnings. If not, you'll need to split the profits with a hired musician. You may also prefer to join forces with other band members and play at weddings, bar and bat mitzvahs, anniversaries, and birthday parties. Look in the trade papers to find like-minded musicians, or enroll with one of the entertainment management firms listed in the yellow pages under "Musician." If you have sight-singing abilities or are extremely proficient with your instrument, studio work might be available. Courses to further your musical training are offered at local community and university adult ed programs.

Salary will vary, depending on your experience and the city

you live in. Ask around to find out the going rates. There are a number of ways to procure work; call the entertainment directors at various facilities to see what they pay, or start volunteering at places that don't pay and keep your business card on hand. Senior centers and retirement homes hire entertainment once a week or once a month, and many nonprofit organizations hire entertainment for their functions. To get a listing of senior centers, contact the department of aging by calling information in your area, or look in the city government listings in your phone book. Also, look in the yellow pages under "Retirement Homes."

Good luck.

- **BENEFITS:** Getting to perform; sharing your music with people; good money.
- **PITFALLS:** Work can be sporadic.
- **SOURCES:** Senior centers and retirement homes. Trade papers. Yellow pages under "Musician" and "Retirement Homes." Department of aging.
- **NEEDS:** Musical abilities; instruments.

4

Do the Locomotion

JOBS FOR PEOPLE WHO
WANT TO KEEP ACTIVE

Aerobics Instructor

Working as an aerobics instructor enables you to maintain an incredible physique while earning some extra money. It is good for your ego since you are a role model for others; you become the leader, the fitness "guru." The shifts are short, the hours are flexible, and the perks generally include free club membership. Best of all, it will keep you motivated to work out when all you really want to do is stay under the covers and eat Häagen-Dazs.

Many clubs require that you be certified, and there are a number of ways and places to do this. The American College of Sports Medicine (ACSM) offers a national aerobics instructor certification exam that costs $220 for members and $270 for nonmembers. Membership provides a career service bulletin. The American Council on Exercise (ACE) also offers an aerobics instructor exam for $200. Once you are certified, ACE will give you a list of gyms and health clubs in your area to help you find employment opportunities. Other certifying organizations include the Aerobics and Fitness Association of America (AFAA), National Academy of Sports Medicine (NASM), the National

Sports Performance Association (NSPA), and National Strength and Conditioning Association (NSCA).

Many fitness centers will accept proof of completion from a local aerobics fitness program instead of these national certificates. Call continuing education programs and community colleges in your area. Many clubs that don't require aerobic certification look to hire studio dancers who know how to create and set up fun, challenging routines and who are experts on the benefits of stretching.

Once you have your instructor certificate, the IDEA Health and Fitness Association, a nineteen-thousand-member organization, provides continuing education, resources, and representation to fitness professionals. You do not have to be certified to become a member, and the group will help you stay certified through independent study courses. Aerobics instructors usually earn between $12 and $65 per class. Some clubs will pay you on commission, so you'll need to fill up your class to make good money.

To apply for a job, contact the aerobics manager at the fitness center that interests you. Then fill out an application and perform your routine. Every major city has many health clubs. Check your local yellow pages under "Health Clubs" for a listing, or get a list through your membership in a certifying organization. Many health clubs have a number of locations, so when calling the numbers provided, ask for the one in your area.

Good luck.

- **BENEFITS:** Staying in great shape; having fun; free membership; flexible shifts.
- **PITFALLS:** Physically demanding if you have many classes.
- **SOURCES:** Classifieds and yellow pages under "Health Clubs." American College of Sports Medicine (ACSM),

317-637-9200, www.acsm.org; certification resource center in Indiana, 800-486-5643; American Council on Exercise (ACE), 800-825-3636, www.acefitness.org; Aerobics and Fitness Association of America (AFAA), 800-446-2322, www.afaa.com; National Academy of Sports Medicine (NASM), 800-460-NASM, www.nasm.org; National Sports Performance Association (NSPA), 301-428-2879; National Strength and Conditioning Association (NSCA), 719-632-6722. IDEA Health and Fitness Association, 800-999-4332, ext. 7. Outside the United States or in Canada, 858-535-8979, ext. 7, www.ideafit.com.

- **NEEDS:** Background in fitness or dance; experience; certification.

Camp Staff

Who doesn't enjoy sitting around a crackling campfire and toasting marshmallows? Fortunately for us, camps aren't just for kids anymore. There are senior citizen camps as well as family, sports, religious, computer, drama, music, tennis, and weight-loss camps, to name a few. All of them need to fill staff positions. Most camps operate in the summer months, but there are also a number of winter camps.

Many college students and teachers find working in a camp extremely complementary to their work schedule. If you have any kind of special skills—lifeguarding, arts and crafts, dance, different sports—you might even be able to run one of the specific departments. Summer camp sessions generally run for eight to ten weeks, with a few additional weeks of preparation involved. There are sleep-over camps and day camps. One day off a week at a sleep-away camp plus a number of evenings off is common.

Working at a camp provides a wonderful social atmosphere.

Working with children and being outdoors, often in rustic environments with a lake and trees, are other pluses. Cons might include having to sleep in a cabin with children if you are an overnight camp counselor.

Wages vary. Expect to earn at least a few hundred dollars a week plus room and board at sleep-away camps. Day camps usually pay a bit higher. Tips from parents on visiting day (at sleep-over camps) can add to your earning potential, especially for counselors. Specialists, program directors, nurses, chefs, and other key staff members have their own sleeping quarters and typically earn higher wages. Another bonus, if you have kids, is free camp for them, which can save you a few thousand dollars!

To get a job at a camp, contact the camp office, which is usually open year-round, or look in the yellow pages under "Camps." Parent magazines are also a good resource, as is the back section of your local paper. Many churches and synagogues have camp programs, and the Jewish Federation, numerous Christian organizations, and the YMCA or YM-YWHA also have many popular summer programs. Almost every state has a YMCA that has camps and its own Web site. Your local chamber of commerce will have listings as well.

Good luck.

- **BENEFITS:** Being outdoors; working with kids; social atmosphere.
- **PITFALLS:** Can be noisy if you're a counselor and sleep in a cabin with kids; the pay isn't terrific for the hours.
- **SOURCES:** Yellow pages under "Camps." Parent magazines. Federations, churches and synagogues, YMCA or YM-YWHA, local chamber of commerce. American Camping Association, 765-342-8456, www.acacamps.org; Summer Camp Employment.com, 800-443-6428, www.summer campemployment.com and www.summercampstaff.com.
- **NEEDS:** Energy and patience; special skill if you want to

teach something specific; enjoyment in working with kids or the target groups.

Construction Work

Construction work varies, depending on your level and experience and abilities. There are basically three levels of work. Day laborers, who do all the grunt work, including mixing cement, installing insulation, and unloading materials and equipment, earn $7 to $12.50 an hour, often with lunch included. Helpers, the next level up, are expected to have an array of tools, including a full nail belt and basic power tools. They are paid approximately $15 to $20 an hour. Finally, journeymen are expected to have table-level power tools; they earn about $30 an hour. It is wise to have health insurance if you're a journeyman since construction jobs can be hazardous.

This is a male-dominated field although there are opportunities for women. Above all, you need to be strong and in good shape since the work is physically demanding. The job is flexible in that you can choose to work only on short-term projects. The hours are typically 7:00 A.M. to 4:00 P.M.

If you're just starting out, you'll need to work as a laborer to gain experience or work as an apprentice. These positions can be found through word of mouth or by simply showing up ready to work at construction sites. One way to find construction sites is to go to city hall to learn where work permits have been pulled. For specific construction jobs, check the classifieds under "Construction" and "Contractor," or contact companies directly by looking in the yellow pages under "Construction" or under specific contractor headings depending on your skills.

Good luck.

• **BENEFITS:** Building muscles and stamina; both outdoor and indoor work available.

- **PITFALLS:** Strenuous physical labor; long hours.
- **SOURCES:** Classifieds and the yellow pages under "Construction" and "Contractor." Word of mouth. City hall for construction sites.
- **NEEDS:** Some experience; strength; physical fitness; tools.

Furniture and Carpet Cleaner

As much as you may not be wild about housekeeping, cleaning carpets and furniture can be a lucrative business. Apartment building owners may have carpets cleaned each time a tenant moves out, and in major cities this happens quite often. Cleaners are also hired for general upkeep and maintenance by apartment renters and homeowners, as well as by restaurants, offices, and corporations.

There are plenty of existing cleaning companies, but this is definitely a profession in which small upstarts thrive. To work for an established business, a responsible, friendly demeanor is needed. Some companies will want experienced cleaners, and some will train you. If you want to start your own business, you will need to purchase an extraction machine. This will handle most of your cleaning needs—carpet shampooing, floor stripping, and most laundering of fabrics. Extra hand tools can be purchased for upholstery, stairs, and stains. It is always a good idea to have the phone number of an established professional cleaning store handy in case you run into problems and need assistance.

There are about six or seven different models of extraction machines to choose from that range in price from $650 to $2,500 (used machines and rentals are also available). Special chemicals must be purchased; these range in price from $3.98 to $20 and cover twenty to thirty jobs. The labels will tell you how each one is used, or someone in the store can explain which products are good for which jobs. Many large-scale janitorial supply stores can be found in the yellow pages under "Janitorial Supplies" and "Carpet, Rug, and Upholstery Cleaning Equipment."

The going rate is approximately 20 to 30 cents per square foot ($55 to $75 for a 250-square-foot room) and about $50 to $80 for a 7-foot sofa. You can charge more for cleaning furniture upholstered with silks, velvets, and other delicate materials because they may require extra work and the use of special cleaners and methods. If you work for a company, you may work on commission; your profit margin will depend on your costs, time, and labor. If you're starting out on your own, call companies in your area for competitive rates. You will need to be insured and bonded. Call insurance agents listed in the yellow pages for rates. A city license or business certificate is also required. Contact your county clerk for information.

The best advertisement is word of mouth. To get your business off the ground, you can post signs at various neighborhood locations, contact apartment managers, take out ads in local newspapers or community papers, and offer special discounted rates to first-time customers and friends, who will refer you to other jobs. Some apartment associations (check under "Apartment Manager," chapter 1) have publications you may advertise in. You can also let management companies and real estate agents, as well as people who remodel homes, know about your service.

Good luck.

- **BENEFITS:** Flexible hours; relatively low initial costs to start your own business.
- **PITFALLS:** Unsteady income; working on commission; need to acquire customers.
- **SOURCES:** Yellow pages. Janitorial supply stores. Apartment magazines. Advertising.
- **NEEDS:** Necessary supplies and equipment; experience.

- **IDEAS:** The same concept can be used for a number of different ventures. Invest in a piece of equipment—snow-plow, lawn mower, floor sander, etc.—and offer your services.

Gourmet Food Delivery

Any urban area will offer a number of gourmet food delivery services, which specialize in delivering prepared foods, often in carts, to office buildings at lunchtime. These services hire independent contractors, supplying you at a highly discounted rate with packaged foods, which you then sell for profit. Because you are responsible for transporting the items you sell, you will need a large cooler for perishables and a car to get from place to place. Companies generally look to hire people who are energetic and friendly, with good marketing abilities, and who are likely to generate regular sales.

After a short training period, most delivery services will let you choose between a five-day existing route, substitute work, and route sharing with another person two to three days a week. The hours are approximately 7:00 A.M. to 2:00 P.M., making this job an ideal opportunity for parents who need to be available to pick up their kids after school. You are usually off on national holidays and the week between Christmas and New Year's. Potential earnings usually range from $65 to $150 per day.

In many cities, catering companies and gourmet food shops also deliver lunches. For a complete listing, look in the yellow pages under "Caterers" and "Gourmet Shops." Visit established office buildings in your area, ask who supplies lunch by cart, and call the numbers. If you have an entrepreneurial spirit and enjoy concocting creative lunch fare, you can even start your own similar service. Present your flyer and menu at businesses around town.

Good luck.

- **BENEFITS:** Independent contracting; shifts ending by early afternoon.
- **PITFALLS:** Early-morning start; money varies with route.
- **SOURCES:** Yellow pages under "Catering" and "Gourmet Shops." Visit established office buildings in your area.
- **NEEDS:** Neat appearance; reliable car with room for a cooler.

Handyman

When I was in college, I had a friend who could fix anything. From toilets to toasters, he was a whiz. He eventually used his talents to help cover the rising cost of his tuition. If you are good with tools and familiar with a variety of appliances, consider being a handyman. There is no end to the number of different jobs you can hire yourself out for. In the past year I have seen advertisements posted around town and even slipped under my door for painting, moving, hauling, carpentry, yard cleanup, electrical work, plumbing, and assemblage work.

If you are skilled in any of these types of service, you can start a business of your own or team up with a partner to increase scheduling flexibility. There are plenty of free places to advertise, including bulletin boards at different organizations, Laundromats, grocery stores, cafés, community papers, and temple or church newsletters. Introduce yourself to building management companies and apartment owners; they always like to be acquainted with someone they can call in a pinch.

The hourly rate for a handyman is usually $10 to $20, depending on the level of skill required. Or you may charge on a per project basis, calculating your prices by hours spent, tools needed, skills required, and equipment purchased. You may also want to consider an apartment management job (see chapter 1) so that you can make good use of your skills and live rent free.

Good luck.

- **BENEFITS:** Self-employment; good wage.
- **PITFALLS:** Unsteady work.
- **SOURCES:** Advertise on bulletin boards around town, in newsletters or community papers. Contact building management companies and apartment owners.
- **NEEDS:** Being a jack-of-all-trades; various tools.

Housecleaning

This job entails exactly what it sounds like: mopping, scrubbing, vacuuming, and dusting specified rooms in other people's homes. It is best suited to those who enjoy working alone or with a partner and don't mind physical labor. Even if you are the type who lets the dust bunnies collect under your bed, don't rule out housekeeping as a possibility. Many people who cannot stand cleaning their own homes actually enjoy cleaning other people's—maybe because they are being paid for it.

Each job requires three to five hours, depending on the size of the residence. You work out the schedule with the owner, and that leaves room for plenty of flexibility. The going rate for housecleaning is $10 to $18 an hour, or you can charge a set price (which may motivate you to work faster). A competitive set rate for cleaning a one-bedroom apartment is $45; a two-bedroom generally brings in $50 to $60. Houses are usually $65 and up, depending on the number of rooms and their sizes. If you bring your own vacuum and cleaning supplies, you can often charge more.

If you choose to work for a service, your wages will be lower, but the service finds the work and sets up your appointments, as many as four per day. The drawback is that the service gets about 50 percent of the job's cost. It is far more lucrative to have your own business and clientele, but you will need to do some basic marketing. You can advertise your services on bulletin boards, in salons, and in specific newspapers; hand out flyers and cards to everyone you know; and offer a first-time discount to people who are well connected and likely to refer you to their friends and associates. It can be helpful to sign on with an existing business first and then head out on your own after you have established a résumé. If you prefer to work for an existing service, check the newspapers and the yellow pages under "Housecleaning" and "Janitorial Service."

Good luck.

- **BENEFITS:** Flexible schedule; good wages.
- **PITFALLS:** Cleaning other people's messes.
- **SOURCES:** Call an existing service, or advertise your own. Check yellow pages under "Housecleaning" and "Janitorial Service."
- **NEEDS:** Responsible and honest character; ability to clean well; cleaning supplies.

Mover

The average person moves approximately ten times in his or her life. The job of a mover is to go to people's homes, carry their belongings out to a truck, drive to a new destination, and unload their things into their new homes. Packers are sometimes hired beforehand to box up the person's belongings. Be warned that this job is physically demanding. Be prepared by bringing a weight belt and gloves. You'll get a great workout, so you can cancel that gym membership!

Movers usually work days or early evenings, with varying shifts. A typical job takes approximately four hours. Most movers are on call, meaning greater flexibility but unsteady work and salary. Income depends on the company you work for and your level of experience. Generally, a mover makes anywhere from $7 to $15 an hour plus tips. A packer, who has experience in wrapping and protecting items, can make closer to $30 an hour.

For specific moving companies in your area, check the yellow pages under "Movers" or the classifieds under "Movers/Drivers."

Good luck.

- **BENEFITS:** Flexible shifts; great physical exercise.
- **PITFALLS:** Physically demanding, unsteady work.
- **SOURCES:** Classifieds and yellow pages under "Movers." A few nationwide companies are Allied Van Lines, Bekins, Starving Students, North American Van Lines, and Moishe's Moving Company. For employment opportunities, contact the branch nearest you.
- **NEEDS:** Excellent physical condition.

Outdoor Wilderness and Teamwork Instructor

Computer gridlock, congestion, smog, boom boxes: Leave them all behind, and become an outdoor wilderness and teamwork instructor. Adventure, majestic scenery, and fun await you in this physically demanding but highly rewarding job. In the field of experiential education, few jobs come close to matching this one in emotional and physical growth. Teachers, parents, students, or anyone with a block of free time will find working as an outdoor wilderness instructor an extremely complementary part-time job. A number of schools handle this training; the best-known is Outward Bound, which has more than forty schools throughout the world and five in the United States. Clients include students, families, camps, and leadership programs, as well as corporations such as Kaiser Permanente, Deloitte & Touche, Rockport, AT&T, and US West.

Wilderness programs are year-round, and activities include mountain climbing, whitewater rafting, canoe paddling, backpacking, rope courses, and problem-solving initiatives. Programs can run anywhere from five to eighty days. Most instructors are hired for two or three courses at a time. The majority of work is in the summer, and some bases provide housing for instructors.

The five Outward Bound schools in the United States work independently. Outdoor experience and good leadership skills are needed to get a paid position. When you are hired, you will complete an initial training session. The school in Maine also hires interns through a program called STEP, which is based in Yulee, Florida. Working as an intern can lead to future paid positions within the Outward Bound schools; you will usually start out as a paid assistant before becoming a full-fledged instructor.

Outward Bound pays $48 to $63 a day for an assistant and $55 to $125 a day for an instructor. Room and board are often covered. For further information, contact the national office of Outward Bound or any of the individual schools. Other organizations in many cities have similar programs on a smaller scale. Check your yellow pages under "Youth Organizations."

Good luck.

- **BENEFITS:** Dynamic training period at the start of the program; getting to be outdoors in some exquisite wilderness; adventures; fun.

- **PITFALLS:** The pay; possible stress from working with kids.
- **SOURCES:** Yellow pages under "Youth Organizations." Outward Bound's national office is 888-882-6863, or visit the Web site at www.outwardbound.com/schoolsctrs. html. At present, the five schools in the United States are: (1) North Carolina Outward Bound, 800-878-5258, www.ncobs.org.; (2) Hurricane Island Outward Bound, in Maine, 800-341-1744, www.hurricaneisland.org.; (3) Pacific Crest Outward Bound, in Portland, Oregon, 800-477-2627, www.pcobs.org.; (4) Voyager Outward Bound, in Minnesota, 800-328-2943, www.vobs.org.; and (5) Colorado Outward Bound, 800-477-2627, www.cobs.org.
- **NEEDS:** Enjoyment of the outdoors; liking kids; patience; handling stress well; ability to motivate others; good physical condition.

Painting Houses

There is always a demand for housepainters. Painting is the least expensive way to improve the look of a home drastically. Anytime someone moves out of an apartment, the management will have it painted for the new tenant, and homeowners trying to sell their houses will often have them painted to attract potential buyers.

Some of the responsibilities of painting houses or apartments include preparing the surfaces by scraping or sanding, covering the furnishings with drop cloths to protect them, and then applying several coats of paint. If you have limited experience, go to the local paint store, and gather all the printed material available to educate yourself on different methods and types of paint. You can then hire yourself out as an apprentice to learn the ropes. It is important to have an eye for color and detail. As with most things, you will become more proficient as you gain experience. The more experience you have, the more money you can make, and eventually you will be able to afford to buy your own tools and start your own business.

Going into business for yourself means advertising your services. Post flyers everywhere, especially around paint and hardware stores. Another good place to advertise is in local papers or at community or religious organizations. As always, word of mouth is the cheapest and best form of advertisement. You will also need to register your business. Call your local city clerk's office, tax and permit division, or county clerk's office. Many customers will ask to see your license. For information on licensing, contact the state contractors' board. I suggest you also get bonded and obtain some kind of liability insurance. Look in your yellow pages under "Insurance," and call for competitive rates.

There is an initial investment in supplies if you go solo. The job requires canvas drop cloths, buckets, brushes, rollers, an extension pole to reach ceilings, ladders, Spackle, Spackle knives, and . . . paint. It is a good idea to establish yourself with a paint supplier so that you will be able to get discounts and return your unused product.

The wage that you can expect as a housepainter depends on what is specifically negotiated with each client before you begin a job. Keep in mind you will need to include the cost of labor and all materials in your price. One simple room at 150 square feet should take you about three to four hours to paint. I was told by experienced painters that if you use middle-grade materials, the net profit will be approximately $125 to $175. A 1,500-square-foot house interior, including ceilings, moldings, and doors, will take about three eight-hour days, and your net profit could be over $2,000. Get everything in writing, and be sure both parties sign the contract. When you work for someone else, the pay is typically $7 to $15 an hour, depending on your experience and how detailed the job is.

Good luck.

- **BENEFITS:** Abundance of jobs; good wages for the self-employed.
- **PITFALLS:** Repetitious, physically demanding work.
- **SOURCES:** Advertising. Work as an apprentice. Referrals. State contractors' board at 800-321-2752.
- **NEEDS:** Painting experience; trustworthiness; dependability. If it is your own business: materials, insurance, a business license, registration, and advertisements.

Personal Trainer

Personal trainers are not the drill sergeants of yesterday. They are highly trained, motivated individuals who assist people in becoming fit and healthy. Many dancers, martial artists, experienced weight lifters, and health-conscious individuals become trainers. Besides the obvious benefit of staying in shape yourself, each personal training session lasts only an hour, making it very easy to create your own schedule.

There are generally two ways to earn money as a personal trainer: Work for a health club, or work privately with your own clientele. The advantage of working in a health club is the stability of hours and clients. The club handles all advertising and equipment costs, free club and spa benefits are included, and you are often allowed to bring in your private clients when you are off the clock.

Most health clubs require you to be certified. The American College of Sports Medicine (ACSM) offers an exam, $220 for members and $270 for nonmembers, that certifies you as a health and fitness instructor. The American Council of Exercise (ACE) also offers a personal trainer exam for $200. Both organizations offer a course of study and a list of recommended readings when they send you the applications for the exams. Other certifying organizations include the Aerobics and Fitness

Association of America (AFAA), National Academy of Sports Medicine (NASM), and National Strength and Conditioning Association (NCSA). Many university extension programs offer certification in fitness training as well. In Los Angeles, UCLA Extension offers such a program, as does New York's Marymount Manhattan College Continuing Education. Once you are certified and working as a trainer, the International Association of Fitness Professionals is a useful organization that provides continuing education, resources, and representation to fitness professionals.

When working at a health club, expect to earn $15 to $30 an hour. As a full-time trainer you can earn between $30,000 and $60,000 yearly. If you work as a private trainer, you will have greater flexibility and earn more money, but you will need to market your skills to gain a regular clientele. Most personal trainers who travel to their clients' homes or gyms charge about $50 to $75 an hour.

If you choose to work independently, good places to advertise for clients might be in a community newsletter or at health and weight-loss establishments. Try giving complimentary or half-price sessions to first-time clients. Let established chiropractors and other health professionals know about your service, and consider a complimentary session in exchange for future referrals. Word of mouth is always the best source. For employment opportunities in health clubs, check the yellow pages under "Health Clubs." One of the largest national health chains, Bally Total Fitness, hires employees on the basis of an interview and the applicants' knowledge of equipment rather than certification. The pay is on the low end, but it can be a good starting point.

Good luck.

- **BENEFITS:** Good pay; being forced to stay in top shape; flexible schedule.
- **PITFALLS:** If you go independent, you'll need to build clientele.
- **SOURCES:** Yellow pages under "Health Clubs." Classifieds. Bally Total Fitness, 800-275-1795, www.ballyfitness.com. American College of Sports Medicine (ACSM), 317-637-9200, www.acsm.org; American Council of Exercise (ACE), 800-825-3636, www.acefitness.org; Aerobics and Fitness Association of America (AFAA), 800-446-2322, www.afaa.com; National Academy of Sports Medicine (NASM), 800-460-NASM, www.nasm.org; National Strength and Conditioning Association (NCSA), 719-632-6722. UCLA Extension, 310-825-9971, www.ucla extension.org. Marymount Manhattan College Continuing Education, 212-517-0400, http://marymount.mmm.edu.; IDEA Health and Fitness Association, 800-999-4332, ext. 7. Outside the United States or Canada, 858-535-8979, ext. 7, www.ideafit.com.
- **NEEDS:** Extensive knowledge of specific exercises and equipment; certification.

Private Mail Carrier

We all know that insurance companies earn the big bucks, so why wouldn't they have their own private mail carrier? Particularly in the insurance industry, there is a tremendous amount of paperwork that needs to be handled carefully and expeditiously. It can't be faxed, and after a while FedEx becomes cost-prohibitive.

As a private mail carrier you do everything that a regular mail carrier does. You are supplied with a vehicle, a uniform, a route, and addresses. There are different shifts available, depending on whether you are a mail carrier, a sorter, or a driver exchanging mail. Typically, a carrier works eight hours, five days a week. Hours can be shorter if you finish your route early. Sorters have somewhat more flexibility, with graveyard shifts and weekend work available. Pay starts at approximately $8 to $10 an hour, with full medical, dental, and health benefits kicking in after ninety days.

To apply for a job, contact private mail carriers, which you can find in the yellow pages under "Mail Carrier" and "Mail Receiving Services." Consider starting your own business by calling your local city or county clerk's office and asking about employment opportunities in your area.

Good luck.

- **BENEFITS:** Unsupervised, no-brainer work.
- **PITFALLS:** Tedious, long hours.
- **SOURCES:** Yellow pages under "Mail Carrier" and "Mail Receiving Services." Local city or county clerk's office.
- **NEEDS:** Being responsible; good physical condition.

Remodeling Homes

Are you a do-it-yourself, fixer-upper kind of person? Does the idea of installing cabinets, tiling, creating moldings, or doing repair work seem as easy to you as boiling water? Then why not earn money with these skills?

There is a tremendous market for home remodeling, composed of people who need to fix up their homes before they sell them or want to improve the houses they live in. People often live twenty-five years in homes without spending much money, and when the time comes to sell, they find they need to do serious work to meet the current building codes, or they decide to beautify their places so they can ask for higher selling prices.

This is where you come in. People are eager to fix up their homes as cheaply and as quickly as possible.

To get a sense of the business, learn the ropes, and build a résumé, I suggest working for a housing contractor. Look in the yellow pages under "Contractor—General." When starting your own business, call your city or county clerk's office for licensing information and insurance companies for public liability and damage insurance as well as bonding. You can hire other professionals if you are too busy or don't want to do certain projects. To find reliable workers, ask for recommendations at hardware stores, paint stores, and building supply companies, found in the yellow pages under "Building Materials." If you have the cash, or connect with a partner who does, you might even consider buying homes that have been repossessed from banks, remodeling them, and selling them for a very nice profit. This can be quite lucrative in areas where real estate is appreciating.

Your earnings will vary greatly. Typically you should give a quote on the whole job, taking into account material costs as well as your hourly rate. Unfortunately, you'll find that people often want to cut corners monetarily but want the work to look expensive. As you learn more about the market, you'll be able to determine your own competitive price. When working for a housing contractor, expect to make about $12 to $25 an hour, depending on your experience.

To find work remodeling houses, advertise in local newspapers (a Pennysaver type of paper) with promotional coupons. Often home and building centers provide bulletin boards for contractor business cards. You can also advertise at your local hardware store and in your community church or temple newsletter or bulletin board. You'll need a business card and information about past work readily available to hand to potential clients. As always, word of mouth is best.

Good luck.

- **BENEFITS:** Being your own boss; flexibility; good wages.
- **PITFALLS:** People often want to hire cheap labor, but they want the work to look expensive.
- **SOURCES:** Advertising in local papers, home and business centers, church and synagogue bulletin boards, hardware stores.
- **NEEDS:** Remodeling skills; tools; knowing reliable workers to hire.

Sports Referee

You always wanted to be on the varsity team as a kid. Or perhaps you were on the team and now want to rekindle those nostalgic feelings. If you are athletic or love sports in general or one sport in particular, being a referee or umpire may be a terrific part-time job for you.

Referees are needed for most sporting events. These include basketball, football, swimming, diving, gymnastics, ice hockey, field hockey, baseball, softball, and track and field. The easiest way to become a referee is to start at the high school level and work your way up. The National Federation of State High School Associates, in Indianapolis, Indiana, for $8, plus shipping and handling, will send you a handbook that lists all the associations across the country, with contact information.

Each state has a high school association that sets its own requirements for youth league, freshmen, junior varsity, and varsity. You'll need to take a rules class, then pass an examination. If officiating at the college level is your preference, you'll probably need to work at the high school level for a few years before applying to the college conference in your area.

To be an umpire at adult games, contact the city hall in your area, and ask for the adult sports department or municipal sports program. There are adult and senior leagues in most cities. To become a ref or umpire at the adult level, you'll also need to pass a test. City hall can refer you to the requisite classes provided by the community in which you live. There is usually minimal or no cost involved.

Salary varies from state to state, depending on your experience and the games you ref. When working for the high school association, you can generally expect to earn $150 to $375 a game. Working for the city, umpiring adult games, pays about $20 cash for an hour game. Not to worry, there are often three games a night! You might also work at sports camps. Check out specific sports papers such as *USA Today Baseball Weekly* for sport camp and workshop opportunities.

A special note: Ladies, don't be shy. This is no longer a men-only club! This could be the perfect job for all you "soccer moms." That way you get to keep an eye on your children and then penalize them when they break the rules. Sweet justice.

Good luck.

- **BENEFITS:** Easy way to stay fit; working with children; being around a sport you enjoy; exciting pace.
- **PITFALLS:** Irate parents and fans; people not agreeing with the officials' calls; can be seasonal.
- **SOURCES:** National Federation of State High School Associates, 317-972-6900, www.nfhs.org. City hall. Sports papers: *USA Today Baseball Weekly*, www.usatoday.com/bbwfront.htm.
- **NEEDS:** Enjoyment of a sport; familiarity with its rules and regulations; ability to make quick decisions; liking kids; passing the examination.

Tennis Umpire

A tennis umpire is the person responsible for making sure the game is played by the rules. This job involves calling the shots, roving on as many as five to ten courts to handle disputes, and calling the score. You move up in the ranks as you gain experience. When first starting out, you will umpire junior, senior, and teen tennis tournaments. As you gain knowledge, experience, and proficiency, you can graduate to umpiring major tournaments, such as Virginia Slims, the L.A. Open, and the U.S. Open.

Wages vary depending on the tournament and the number of hours worked. A 6-love, 6-1 match can get you off court in as little as forty-five minutes. Other days you may be on the court for as long as ten hours (with breaks in between, of course). You typically earn anywhere from $70 to $150 a day. Hours are flexible since you can choose the jobs that fit your schedule. The work is primarily on weekends and sometimes in the evenings.

The United States Tennis Association (USTA) main headquarters is in White Plains, New York, and you can call for a referral number in your region. Basically, all the associations work in a similar manner. They hold a basic training umpire school a few times per year. The course is one full day and costs $15 to $20. This fee covers the cost of parking, breakfast, lunch, and a copy of *Friends at Court*, the USTA official handbook. In the morning you'll go over the rules of tennis. In the afternoon there will be an on-court session with tennis players approximating a match and a no-fail exam given at the end of the day (my kind of exam). In other words, if you fail with the handbook closed, you can open it up, fill in the answers quoting the book, self-correct, and pass.

Good luck.

- **BENEFITS:** Fun; meeting people; learning about tennis.
- **PITFALLS:** People yelling, "Kill the ump."
- **SOURCES:** United States Tennis Association, 914-696-7000, www.usta.com. Call the Southern California Tennis

Association, 310-208-3838; Northern California Association, 510-748-7373; Mid-Atlantic Office, 703-560-9480; Pacific Northwest Section, 503-520-1877; Midwest Section, 317-577-5130; and Florida Section, 386-671-8949.

- **NEEDS:** Love of tennis; responsible character; fairness; knowledge of rules; passing an examination.

Wallpapering

Hanging wallpaper may be a skill you already have from decorating your own apartment or seeing your folks do it. If you don't already know how to hang wallpaper, you can learn this valuable skill by practicing on your own walls (it's always a good time to redecorate) or becoming an apprentice to a more experienced paperhanger. By learning the tricks of the trade—for example, metallic paper once creased is creased for good, and grass cloth doesn't require a match—you can be well on your way to earning a decent hourly wage.

Paperhangers size up the rooms they are hanging and prepare the surfaces so the wallpaper will stick better. To gather tools, such as sponges, drop cloths, a ladder, and buckets, go to a supply store. Paperhangers often work closely with interior decorators, found in the yellow pages under "Interior Decorators and Designers." To apprentice, look up "Paperhangers" in the yellow pages.

Being in good physical condition and having manual dexterity will come in handy. This job requires standing for long periods of time. It is also important to be comfortable on a ladder and have the ability to work patiently by yourself for a number of hours, possibly all day, in one room.

Pay will vary. It's customary to charge per roll of paper used. It usually takes about twenty minutes to hang a roll. Cost may also depend on the room. A bathroom will typically cost more because there are a number of fixtures to remove and shorter walls. A job usually pays about $450 to $650 for a few days' work. Call wallpaper hangers in your area for competitive rates.

If you are not working with an established company, word of mouth is the best way to get work. Advertise or leave business cards in neighborhood stores, and try to contact local decorators for referrals. The International Union of Painters and Allied Trades or the Joint Apprenticeship Training Fund can connect you with local unions, give professional training, and certify workers. For nonunion apprentice programs, go through contracting companies listed in the yellow pages under "Wall Covering Contractors," "Interior Decorators and Designers," and "Paperhangers."

Good luck.

- **BENEFITS:** If independent, you can control your own time and be your own boss; being creative; immediate results; good wages.
- **PITFALLS:** Physically challenging, tedious work.
- **SOURCES:** Word of mouth. Advertising. Local decorators. International Union of Painters and Allied Trades, 800-437-7347, www.iupat.org; Joint Apprenticeship Training Fund (JATF), 800-276-7289. Yellow pages under "Wall Covering Contractors," "Interior Decorators and Designers," and "Paperhangers."
- **NEEDS:** Tools and ladder; experience.

Working in a Health Club

Today just about everyone belongs to a health club. Why wouldn't he or she want to? Health clubs are the places to tone up, lose weight, destress, get massages, make friends, or even meet future spouses. Working at a health club is a great way to take advantage of all these perks—and make money!

Health clubs offer various employment opportunities. Receptionists answer phones, salespeople sell memberships, floor managers make sure the club is running well on a daily basis, lifeguards work at the club's pool, and counter people work at the health bar. If you're a hard-core fitness buff, you may want to try your hand at being a personal trainer or aerobics instructor (see sections in this chapter). For those less physically inclined, there are plenty of other options. If you have good verbal skills and an outgoing personality, you are a natural to work in a health club atmosphere. Working in a health club supports your efforts to stay in top shape. Facilities are at your disposal, and all those great bodies walking around will keep you on your toes. No more Twinkies! Since health clubs are open early in the morning until late in the evening and on weekends, a variety of shifts is available.

Starting wages for counter jobs and receptionists typically range from $7 to $10 an hour and include free club membership. Salespeople also receive commissions for enrolling new members. For employment opportunities, check the yellow pages under "Health Clubs." Many clubs have a number of locations, so when you call the numbers provided, ask for the one in your area. One of the largest national chains is Bally Total Fitness, which has fitness centers all over the country.

Good luck.

- **BENEFITS:** Use of club and spa; incentive to keep in shape; energetic atmosphere; meeting people.
- **PITFALLS:** Low starting wage.
- **SOURCES:** Yellow pages under "Health Clubs." Bally Total Fitness, 800-275-1795, www.ballyfitness.com.
- **NEEDS:** Communication skills; friendliness; outgoing personality; energy!

Yoga Teacher

If you enjoy yoga and practice it regularly, becoming a yoga teacher may be a great way for you to enjoy this spiritual form of exercise while making money. In addition to earning money, you will save it if you are currently paying to take classes.

You will probably want to choose a specific type of yoga on which to concentrate. Some gyms offer generic yoga classes, but most classes are taught in a particular style. The six most popular forms of hatha yoga that are being practiced in gyms, yoga studios, and health centers across the United States are: (1) ashtanga; (2) power (vinyasa); (3) bikram; (4) iyengar; (5) kripalu; and (6) kundalini. You will find classes simply called hatha yoga, which may incorporate several more specific kinds of hatha yoga. If you are undecided on a focus, you might want to read a book on a particular style. Some helpful books are *Ashtanga Yoga: The Practice Manual*, by John Scott and Shri K. Pattabhi Jois; *Yoga the Iyengar Way: The New Definitive Illustrated Guide*, by Silva Mehta, et al.; and *Power Yoga: The Total Strength and Flexibility Workout*, by Beryl Bender Birch. Try local bookstores or Amazon.com.

You will need to undergo some kind of teacher training to get hired at most studios, and having some kind of certification will no doubt help you promote your own class if you go that route. There are teacher-training courses offered across the country, and all around the world, as this Eastern practice that combines meditation and movement grows ever more popular. Reputable schools can be found through the Yoga Alliance and *Yoga Journal* on-line, which have comprehensive lists of schools that offer teacher-training programs. Some schools are Kripalu in New England, Dharma Yoga Studio in California, and Yoga Teacher Training Institute in New York. Kripalu offers a two-hundred-hour "Basic Certification" and a five-hundred-hour

"Professional-Level Certification." Its two-hundred-hour certification is offered in a twenty-eight-day format for as little as $1,652, or about $2,800 including room and board. Most two-hundred-hour trainings will cost you between $1,200 and $3,000, depending on what is included. Most studios will want you to have at least two to five hundred hours of training before you teach.

A gym or a yoga studio is often the best place to begin teaching. In most cities there are numerous yoga studios, and many towns now have local holistic health centers that offer yoga classes. You can make a decent income with a flexible schedule, working part- or full-time. Most places pay you either a flat fee per class, usually around $30 to $40, or a percentage. If paid a percentage, you would typically earn about 40 to 60 percent of what the students pay. At a popular studio that pays by this method, you could expect to earn $100 for a ninety-minute class. When looking for work, check with your local gym, or look in the yellow pages under "Yoga Instruction" for yoga studios. Most of the teacher-training schools offer yoga classes for all levels and are places where you could potentially work.

If you want to start your own class, studio space is usually available for a flat fee, though the owner might request a percentage. For example, you could be asked to pay a flat fee of thirty dollars for the space. If you have ten students, and you charge $10 each, you will earn $70 for a class, which usually runs ninety minutes. Most yoga classes run between $7 to $15, so it's a good idea to stay within that range. If you have good marketing skills, and you have developed a clientele, you may decide to start your own studio. Post flyers in places like the local health food store, vitamin stores, universities, bookstores, and doctors' offices or hospitals that will allow it. Be sure to place the flyers near your yoga space, for people will be more apt to give a class a try if it's in their neighborhood.

Good luck.

- **BENEFITS:** Substantial income; learning as you teach; contributing to people's health; staying in shape; flexible schedule; no equipment to invest in.
- **PITFALLS:** Tuition; building clientele; physically demanding if you have many classes.
- **SOURCES:** New York: Om Yoga Center, 212-254-YOGA, www.omyoga.com; Yoga Teacher Training Institute, 631-543-7490, www.teachyoga.org. New England: Kripalu, 413-448-3327, www.kripalu.org. California: Dharma Yoga Studio, 415-924-8881, www.dharmayoga.org; Yoga Research and Education Center, Santa Rosa, 707-566-9000, www.yrec.org. Chicago: Eight Limbs Yoga Center, 773-561-1877, www.eightlimbs.com. National Information: Yoga Alliance, www.yogaalliance.org, 877-964-2255; *Yoga Journal*, www.yogajournal.com. Contact your local gym or health center. Search the Internet, or check the yellow pages under "Yoga Instruction."
- **NEEDS:** Interest in yoga; training and certification; patience.

5

Don't Be Shy

WINNING PERSONALITY JOBS

Artist's Model

If you are uninhibited, comfortable with posing, enjoy silence, and able to remain still for about twenty minutes, modeling for artists may be a good part-time job for you. Models are employed by drawing classes and professional artists to pose nude or partially nude. Many art schools have model-hiring departments, and instructors have specific model books. You will often need to send in a résumé, including any previous modeling work; your measurements; and a few photos of yourself, nude or clothed.

A typical session involves posing in a single position anywhere from twenty minutes to three hours, with short breaks. The reward, besides monetary, is seeing yourself in a drawing or sculpture. It also feels good to know you have helped artists in their work. The pay is around $10 to $20 an hour.

For employment opportunities, contact art schools or the art departments of colleges and universities in your area. To get work independently, you can post notices on bulletin boards at schools with solid art departments or at independent drawing schools.

Good luck.

- **BENEFITS:** Helping artists; seeing yourself in paintings; working whenever you're available.
- **PITFALLS:** Stiffness of joints; boredom if you're not the silent, contemplative type; no pockets for tips!
- **SOURCES:** Contact art and photography schools.
- **NEEDS:** Comfort with nudity and posing; ability to remain still; good bladder control!

Audience Recruiting, Booking, and Coordinating

Turn on the TV, and you will hear audiences laughing, asking questions, or, if it's an infomercial, trying a product. Talk shows, infomercials, pilots, and sitcoms hire part-time freelance people who are good at promotion and sales to manage such audiences. There are a variety of positions available, including audience recruiters, audience bookers, and audience coordinators. Being outgoing, organized, and personable is the sought-after quality for these positions. A person I know has been involved in all these capacities at one time or another. He has made excellent money and found the work fun, flexible, and a great way to meet people. For someone interested in pursuing a job in TV or related fields, these jobs can also be a good way to make important industry contacts.

AUDIENCE RECRUITERS

Audience recruiters are responsible for going out into the streets, malls, theaters, concerts, parties, and anywhere else that people congregate to hand out passes or tickets for a particular show. The tickets are coded, and you are paid by how many people show up. Pay usually ranges from $6 to $12 a head, although it can be higher if it's a project that the audience will actually be involved in. The law of averages states that about 10 percent of all the people you approach will show up. It goes without saying that the percentage is higher if the show features a spectacular guest.

AUDIENCE BOOKERS

Audience bookers are in charge of booking groups (college clubs, social groups) over the telephone to come to shows. Groups are essential to a show's success. Wages vary depending on the studio, but the booker usually makes $60 to $100 per show. Full-time workers in this area can make salaries of $500 and up a week.

AUDIENCE COORDINATORS

Audience coordinators are responsible for placing audience members in seats. This may not seem important, but balance in terms of ethnicity, age, and sex reflects a show's values. Once again, income will vary. Full-time workers can make anywhere from $500 to $1,200 a week, while freelance workers can earn $60 to $100 per show.

As usual, having contacts is the best way to get one of these positions. Another way is to look in *TV Guide* to see what's being taped in your area and to call those specific studios. Ask for the audience relations department, and stress any promotional experience you have. Performing arts bookstores are still another source; they have books with updated information on shows currently being taped and the studios that produce them.

Good luck.

- **BENEFITS:** Fun; meeting people; making industry contacts.
- **PITFALLS:** Freelance jobs equal unsteady money; shows are sometimes canceled.
- **SOURCES:** Contacts. Audience relations department of studios. *TV Guide*. Performing arts bookstores.
- **NEEDS:** Chutzpah; previous promotional experience.

City Tour Guide

A tour guide gives a factual and comprehensive history and bits of trivia about various city sites while riding on a tourist bus or private coach. Tours can range from three hours to a full day. Depending on your city, trips can include local beaches, zoos, famous sites, and the ever-popular celebrity homes.

This job is especially good for a person who knows his or her city extremely well, remembers funny stories and facts, has many hobbies and diverse interests, is familiar with a variety of local restaurants, and speaks more than one language. To be hired as a guide, you must enjoy talking and have good inter-personal skills. A good tour is really a type of performance, so the ability to improvise is also helpful.

Part-time, full-time, or freelance work is available, as well as weekend work, depending on the company. There are many advantages to this job: meeting people from around the world, seeing different locations, performing for audiences, and, if you choose to develop your own tour business, being your own boss. Depending on your city and experience, salary will range from $7 to $20 an hour, plus tips, which are usually shared with the driver.

A number of travel departments at community colleges offer tour guide courses and help you find employment upon completion. For example, West L.A. College's travel department offers a tour escorting and planning program. The program meets once a week for eighteen weeks. In certain cities, such as New York, a tour guide license is required. A license can usually be purchased for a nominal fee from the New York City Department of Consumer Affairs, after you have passed an exam determining your knowledge of the city. A tour guide publication specific to your city is an excellent resource to help you study. Michelin Travel Publications publishes tour guide and travel books for most major cities.

For employment opportunities, look in the local yellow pages under "Tours—Operators and Promoters." Allied Tours has offices in New York, Los Angeles, Miami, Orlando, Montreal, and Honolulu. About America Tours offers tours in New York, Washington, D.C., Boston, and Niagara Falls. There are numerous smaller companies as well. If you wish to start your own freelance business, check out the book *Start and Run a Profitable Tour Guiding Business,* by B. Braidwood, S. Boyce, and R. Cropp. Try local bookstores or Amazon.com.

Good luck.

- **BENEFITS:** Meeting a variety of people; learning about your city; getting to use your foreign languages.
- **PITFALLS:** Some companies require you to work a few tours in a day.
- **SOURCES:** Yellow pages under "Tours—Operators and Promoters." Travel departments at community colleges. In New York, call the Department of Consumer Affairs, 212-487-4161. Michelin Travel Publications, 800-423-0485. Allied Tours, www.alliedtpro.com, in New York, 212-869-5100; Los Angeles, 310-289-8776; Miami, 305-673-8776; Orlando, 407-934-8776; Honolulu, 808-924-0400; and Montreal, 514-499-3634.
- **NEEDS:** Good people skills; affinity for trivia; excellent knowledge of your city; a license in some cities.

Custom-Made Closets

Organizing, designing, and installing closets have been a thriving (if little-known) business for a number of years. It all started when Imelda Marcos opened a closet door and hundreds of shoes tumbled down on her. . . .

A customer who calls a closet company is given an appointment for a free consultation. You, the salesperson and designer, go to the home, find out what the customer's goals are, take measurements, figure out a workable design, and give a price quote. You then drop off your assessment plans, and a company installer will put the closet together and handle the rest of the deal.

This job is perfect for someone who has a flair for design and interior decorating. Keep in mind, though, that the emphasis here is on sales. You need to convince your customers of the merit of your designs and urge them to go forward with the actual installations. Working for a closet company can be both flexible and lucrative. You tell the company what your schedule is, and it sets up appointments accordingly. A consultation usually takes thirty to sixty minutes, and of course, travel time is involved.

Most closet companies hire salespeople to work on commission, with corporate benefits after three months. Your commission is typically 8 to 12 percent of the job. The jobs usually range from $400 to $10,000. If you work part-time, it's not uncommon to pull in $400 a week or more. Since it is commission-based, the more time and energy you put into it, the more money you'll earn. The average company closing ratio is one in two jobs.

There is initially one week of required training and then sales meetings a few times a month. For more information on employment opportunities, check the yellow pages under "Closets," or look in the classifieds. Closet World services all of Southern California. Closet Factory services a number of areas and cities around the country.

Good luck.

• **BENEFITS:** Setting your own schedule; good wage potential.

- **PITFALLS:** Commission means unsteady salary; people not showing up for appointments.
- **SOURCES:** Yellow pages under "Closets." Classifieds. Closet World, www.closetworld.com, 800-452-5673, services all of Southern California. Closet Factory, www.closetfactory.com, 310-715-1000, 800-318-8800, services a number of areas around the country.
- **NEEDS:** Helpfulness; friendly demeanor; sales experience preferred.

1-800-DENTIST

I'm sure many of you have seen those friendly commercials for 1-800-DENTIST, but I'll bet you weren't aware that congenial, outgoing individuals actually handle the calls. These operators assist people in finding the appropriate dentist, depending on special needs, location, insurance, and orthodontal requirements. 1-800-DENTIST is now servicing about thirty states, with the main corporate office in California. At the time of this book's publication, hiring is done only in New Jersey and California.

This is the way the system works: Dentists pay a fee to become members. They are screened by the company and checked for references and reputation, and they are eliminated from the list if there are any complaints. Upon company approval, the names of dentists and their office locations are programmed into the computer.

As a customer service operator you work loosely from a script, having basic points to cover when people call in. You then determine what type of dentist is needed and give your caller the background and qualifications of the selected dentist. This job requires a combination of phone operator skills and customer service and sales skills. Basic computer know-how and a personable, patient, and courteous manner are musts. It is a flexible job in that you can switch shifts freely or leave early if it's slow. Shifts are from five to seven hours, and most employees work twenty-five to thirty hours a week. A masseuse, hired by the company, comes in once a week and gives everyone a fifteen-minute neck and shoulder massage (sounds as if this company knows how to take care of its employees!).

Starting salary is $8 an hour. Raises of up to 75 cents an hour after each ninety-day period, based on performance, attendance, and attitude, are available. The company gives frequent bonuses for a variety of reasons, such as quotas being reached, incoming calls being turned into referrals, and maintaining a great attitude. To apply for a job, call 201-843-2144, and ask for the human resources or personnel department.

Good luck.

- **BENEFITS:** Flexible shifts; sitting down; bonuses; weekly massage.
- **PITFALLS:** Can be tedious.
- **SOURCES:** Call 201-843-2144, www.1800dentist.com, www.futuredontics.com.
- **NEEDS:** Basic computer skills; personable, courteous, and professional speaking voice.

Direct Marketing of Cosmetics

No doubt you have heard of Avon cosmetics or have seen that prized pink Mary Kay Cadillac cruising around, but did you know how lucrative it can be to work for one of these companies? Mary Kay Inc. is not only the number one selling cosmetics company but one of the esteemed Fortune 500 companies and one of the ten best companies for women to work for. There are more than nine hundred thousand consultants nationwide. You are not restricted to a particular selling area, so you can sell the product line anywhere at any time. Both Avon and Mary Kay allow their products to be sold through any number of channels: parties, setting up shop, or even door to door.

The job can be very flexible since your earnings depend on your efforts. You need to market your products by networking with others, and you are paid up to 50 percent of everything you sell, plus bonuses. An actress I know offers free facials and makeovers to inspire people to test the products. New products come out every year, and they are advertised in such magazines as *Better Homes and Gardens* and *New Woman.* This is a great advertising tool, and you don't have to pay for it. Mary Kay and Avon offer free skin care classes to teach consultants about the new lines.

For further information, call Mary Kay and Avon. They will then refer you to a senior consultant in your area who will show you the ropes. There are other cosmetic companies to work for as well. Look in your local yellow pages under "Cosmetics—Retail."

Good luck.

- **BENEFITS:** Flexible hours; meeting people; reorders; learning about makeup and skin care; bonuses.
- **PITFALLS:** Unsteady income; working on commission.
- **SOURCES:** Yellow pages under "Cosmetics—Retail." Mary Kay, 800-627-9529, www.marykay.com. Avon, 800-858-8000, www.avon.com. For more information on direct selling, contact the Direct Selling Association, 202-347-8866, www.dsa.org.
- **NEEDS:** Outgoing, upbeat personality; networking abilities.

Food Demonstrator

Presenting a specific food product to the public and giving out free samples to increase product awareness and sales are a great job for outgoing Benihana wanna-bes. Demos occur at peak shopping hours, on the weekends, or early evenings during the week. Grocery stores, specialty food shops, and malls are the most popular places for presenting food. Different locations and free product leftovers are key advantages of this job.

Most employees work two to three shifts a week, and shifts usually last four to six hours. Employees of all ages are hired, and many demo businesses will hire and train you over the phone, cutting down on your travel time. Owning a car is a must since locations vary. Some companies will send you out only within ten miles of your home if you request it. Certain companies expect you to supply your own appliances (such as a blender or skillet) to demonstrate a product. Be aware that some jobs may require slightly more physical work if you need to lift cartons, crates, or heavy food items. Pay ranges from $7 to $12 an hour. Most small, local agencies pay the lower hourly wage. To obtain a higher wage, seek employment directly from gourmet or specialty food stores. Some companies also provide mileage and drive time compensation.

For employment, contact different food demo businesses listed in the business-to-business yellow pages, under "Demonstration Service Merchandise." Ask for the supervisor in your area. Demo Deluxe services all California, Idaho, Utah, Oregon, Washington, Nevada, Arizona, and New Mexico. A national company serving the entire country is FoodTemps, which pays $8 to $10 an hour and is the official agency that supplies demonstrators for the Fancy Food Industry Trade Show held two times a year on both the East and West coasts. Yet another way to gain employment is to approach demonstrators you see working in local stores and ask them who they work for.

Good luck.

- **BENEFITS:** Flexible hours; weekend and evening work; left-over food.
- **PITFALLS:** Tedious work; having to stand.
- **SOURCES:** Demo marketing companies. Demo Deluxe, 714-974-1700. FoodTemps, 800-231-9090. Business-to-business yellow pages under "Demonstration Service Merchandise."
- **NEEDS:** Outgoing personality; good grooming; love or knowledge of food.

Fragrance Model

Erase the memory of your mother struggling to avoid the spray of perfume as she walked through department stores dragging you behind her. Today being a fragrance model means something different. You no longer have to accost people aggressively with bottles of strong-scented perfume. In fact, fragrance companies prefer that you not be too pushy. The objective of a fragrance model is to get the word out on a new perfume. The job entails spraying perfume on a card and asking shoppers if they would like to try a new fragrance. Outgoing, personable people with a good sense of style are hired for this position. Fragrance modeling is a freelance position. Shifts run for about four hours, and wages are usually $10 to $15 an hour, depending on your experience and whether you work directly for a fragrance company or through an agency.

Employment as a fragrance model can be secured in a variety of ways. You can go directly to fragrance counters in department stores in your area and ask for information. Call human resources at different perfume manufacturers. Also, frequent department stores on the weekends, and ask the fragrance models for contact numbers.

Good luck.

- **BENEFITS:** Good hourly wage; meeting people; smelling nice.
- **PITFALLS:** Having to stand; pressure to sell; unsteady work.
- **SOURCES:** Fragrance counters at department stores. Human resource department of perfume companies. Fragrance models for contact numbers.
- **NEEDS:** Being outgoing and personable; sense of style.

Fundraising

Universities, foundations, and many nonprofit companies and organizations hire staffs to help raise funds. Universities typically employ students to work in their development offices contacting alumni. This job is especially beneficial, as students get to see what others have done with their degrees. Fundraising parties and free admission to museums and other nonprofit organizations are some of the perks.

Telemarketing, data entry, and face-to-face solicitation are a few of the part-time, flexible fundraising positions. Weekend and evening hours are available. Telemarketers solicit contributions, and data entry employees input the data telemarketers receive, plus mailing lists and other pertinent information. Face-to-face solicitors set up meetings and work to get funds donated. Successful fundraising requires persuasive skills, tenacity, and a friendly, professional attitude. You learn how to ask for what you want, an ability that will serve you well in different arenas of life.

Pay scale varies, but it is usually a base salary plus a commission dependent on the amount of pledges that come in. Expect an hourly wage of $7 to $20. Data entry people make about $10 to $18 an hour depending on the city. Part-time in-person fundraisers make about $25,000 to $30,000 a year.

To get a job in fundraising, go to the development office at your university or call different foundations. Look in the yellow pages under "Foundations—Educational, Philanthropic, Research, Etc." Most large cities have foundation centers (call information for the one in your city). Your library has a book called *The Foundation Directory*, which is an excellent resource tool, or use the Internet to look up nonprofit organizations. Choose one of the many search engines available, such as Google, and type in "nonprofit organizations."

Good luck.

- **BENEFITS:** Fundraising parties; learning persuasive skills; flexible hours; free admission to museums; making contacts.
- **PITFALLS:** Dealing with rejection.
- **SOURCES:** Universities. Nonprofit organizations. Hospitals. The Foundation Center in New York, 212-620-4230, 800-424-9836, http://fdncenter.org. Yellow pages under "Foundations—Educational, Philanthropic, Research, Etc." Your library has a book called *The Foundation Directory*.
- **NEEDS:** Persuasive, friendly demeanor; professional attitude.

Hairstylist

You don't have to be José Eber to earn money cutting and styling hair. Many salons hire part-time hairstylists to work day, evening, or weekend shifts. Also, quite a number of hairstylists go to people's homes and work on a freelance basis. Job description may include shampooing, cutting, and styling hair, as well as perming, straightening, highlighting or dyeing hair, and even styling wigs and hairpieces. It is extremely important to keep on top or ahead of styles and trends.

To start off, you need to be licensed through the state board of cosmetology (which costs only about $30); call information in your area for the phone number. Typically, you must complete sixteen hundred to two thousand hours of beauty school, along with a theory and practical test. This will take anywhere from eight months to a year and a half, depending on whether you attend part-time or full-time. Beauty school generally costs a few thousand dollars, and the school will often handle licensing matters for you. To obtain a license, you must pass practical and written exams. Primarily, sanitary measures are emphasized in these exams because you will learn most of the specific techniques of hairstyling after schooling when you are employed as an assistant at a good salon. Beauty schools are listed in the yellow pages and often in the classifieds. Some universities also offer training. You will need to renew your license every one or two years, and it usually costs around $30 to $40.

Salary varies, depending on whether you rent a station at a salon and provide most of your own clientele or work for a salon. If you rent a station, expect to pay about $50 to $75 for the day and to earn $25 to $50 an hour according to how busy you are. At a salon where you are hired as an employee, you can expect to keep a commission of 60 percent plus tips; expect to earn $9 to $20 an hour. The busier you are in either case, the more money you make. So a friendly demeanor is just as important as talent. To get a job, network with other hairstylists, look in the classifieds under "Beauty Salons," and walk into salons and ask if they are hiring.

Good luck.

- **BENEFITS:** Creative freedom; self-expression; meeting people; using haircuts to barter for other things.
- **PITFALLS:** Slow periods; trying to build a clientele; having to stand.
- **SOURCES:** Classifieds. Yellow pages under "Beauty Sa-

lons." Network with other hairstylists and neighborhood salons. National Cosmetology Association, www.salon professionals.org. For a comprehensive list of beauty schools in the United States, visit www.beautyschool.com. For information on state licensing in Chicago, 217-785-0800, www.dpr.state.il.us; in New York, http://licensing @dos.state.ny.us; in California, 916-323-9020, www.dca.ca.gov/barber/licensing.htm; in Washington, D.C., District of Columbia Board of Cosmetology, 202-442-4320; in Boston, 617-727-9940.

- **NEEDS:** Knowledge of latest trends; cosmetologist license.

Handing Out Movie Passes

I'm sure at one time or another in Los Angeles or New York you have been approached by someone with a stack of flyers in hand, asking if you wanted to attend a free movie screening. What you probably haven't known is that these people work for a company that does market research on films before their commercial release.

Outgoing, assertive people are hired for this job. You pick up a packet that includes approximately fifty tickets, and you have twenty-four hours to return it. The job is flexible in that you choose your own hours, but companies generally prefer a four-day-a-week commitment. You are given a spec on the type of audience required in terms of age, sex, and ethnicity, and then you seek out people accordingly. The ease of this job will depend on the type of movie you are "selling" and the lead actors. One of the common disadvantages is being assigned to an inconvenient area. Also, you may have certain quotas to fill in terms of audience selection. It usually takes between three and five hours to hand out all the flyers.

You are paid by how many people on the list you turn in actually show up for the screening. The company keeps track of this information, and if five people show up, you typically earn $50. If ten people show up, you earn $75. If fifteen show up, you earn $100, and after that you earn $3 to $5 a person. If you see someone handing out these flyers, ask him or her for the number of the company. In California, call National Research Group, and in New York and New Jersey, call Matrix Alliance Market Research.

Good luck.

- **BENEFITS:** Flexible hours; good earning potential.
- **PITFALLS:** Unsteady salary; having to approach strangers; specific quotas to be filled; bad locations.
- **SOURCES:** Ask a person who is handing out these passes for a contact number. National Research Group (NRG), 800-AJOBNOW. Matrix Alliance Market Research, 203-698-3344 or 888-777-3360.
- **NEEDS:** A reliable car for Los Angeles; outgoing, assertive, personable personality.

Makeup Artist

If you enjoy working with people on a one-to-one basis and helping them look their best, becoming a freelance makeup artist can be a fun, challenging, and lucrative way to use your creative talents. Makeup artists are hired for all sorts of social events, such as charity functions, weddings, and fashion shows, and for films and TV shows. A talent for makeup application as well as an understanding of people's features and needs is required. It is also important to be a good communicator.

There are many ways to become a makeup artist. Image consulting and makeup classes are offered through beauty and continuing education schools, or you can look in the classifieds under "Schools/Colleges—Artist." The least expensive way to get started is by working with a major cosmetic line at a department store. Clinique, Estée Lauder, Lancôme, Prescriptives, Bobbi Brown, and Chanel are a few popular lines. If you stay with a line long enough, you will learn the art of makeup application. Makeup seminars are periodically offered to enhance one's skills.

While I was a student at New York University, I worked with Clinique as a freelance "associate consultant" (I've recently met a number of women who are working this same job). It was a great part-time job. I earned good money, learned a lot about makeup application, and received free makeup (my friends and family loved that part!). Freelance consultants work the promotions (including makeovers) at various department stores. For information on this type of position, contact human resources at various cosmetic lines. You can expect to earn about $10 to $15 an hour. Outside the department store, makeup artists can make excellent money. In major cities the fee for an hour of makeup application in a person's home is typically $50 to $125 and up. Makeup artists who work for photographers charge $50 to $100 an application.

Many studios and hair salons hire freelance makeup artists. Check the yellow pages under "Makeup and Beauty Consultants" and "Beauty Salons." You can also advertise your services in the trade papers, local papers, and community newsletters and at salons and health clubs.

Good luck.

- **BENEFITS:** Good money; artistic outlet; helping people look and feel better; free makeup.
- **PITFALLS:** Can be a lengthy process to become skilled and earn steady money.
- **SOURCES:** Makeup schools, department stores, and stu-

dios. Beauty and continuing education schools. Classifieds under "Schools/Colleges—Artist." Yellow pages under "Makeup and Beauty Consultants" and "Beauty Salons." Yellow pages under "Photographers" or the trades *(Backstage, Dramalogue, Variety, Hollywood Reporter)* and *The Working Actors Guide,* published by Aaron Blake. Advertise your services in the trade papers, local papers, and community newsletters and at salons and health clubs.

- **NEEDS:** Talent for applying makeup; enjoyment of working with people on one-to-one basis.

Modeling

While modeling is often a career in itself, it can also be done part-time while you pursue other options. There is a misconception that you need to be "model beautiful" to work. Many advertisers these days are using real people and character types, not to mention fit models and specific body part models.

Modeling can include any of the following: print work for newspapers, magazines, billboards, and catalogs; runway work, which involves showing the product by walking down a runway in front of an audience; and showroom work, which entails wearing different samples of the product for potential buyers. The manufacturer or designer will often hire a showroom model with specific measurements (they vary with each line) to present the product to department store representatives or other buyers. Designers and clothing manufacturers also hire fit models to try on their clothes. Fit models are needed for most sizes if you have the perfect measurements. To find out if you are eligible, contact a design center or manufacturer listed in the yellow pages under "Designers—Apparel."

If you have beautiful hands and well-groomed nails (women's glove size of 6½ to 7½, ring size 4½ to 5½; men's glove size 8½ to 10), or if you have a model shoe size (women's 6 with a narrow or medium width, men's size 9 to 10), being a hand or shoe model is extremely lucrative.

Modeling hours vary. Go-see appointments for print modeling are the equivalent of auditions and are scheduled mainly on weekdays. The more appointments, the more possibilities of booking jobs—just like acting. Modeling provides the opportunity to make a lot of money for relatively short hours, and you are often sent on location to shoot; this offers variety and adventure. On the downside, it is very competitive, and you may have to go on many go-sees to book work. For hand and feet models, an agent usually submits a picture to book a job directly.

To get go-see appointments, you need a good agent. Most modeling agents will accept snapshots of you for consideration and have open calls one day a week. If you call an agency and it will not set up an appointment, you can always stop by to drop off pictures or send a few in the mail. Needs change daily within agencies, and timing is everything.

After you have secured an agent, you will need professional photos and a zed card, which is a 5½-by-8½ composite. It usually has three photos on one side and one photo on the other, with measurements. To obtain a zed card, contact theatrical headshot photographers listed in the yellow pages under "Photographers" and specific trade papers (*Dramalogue* and *Backstage*). Local theatrical agencies (listed in your yellow pages) can also assist you with contact numbers of photographers.

Salary for modeling is open for negotiation. Print modeling pays about $250 an hour. Call the Screen Actors Guild (SAG) and American Federation of Television and Radio Artists (AFTRA) for fee schedules for union work. The low end for fit modeling is about $60 an hour.

Modeling agencies are listed in the yellow pages. Performing arts bookstores carry updated books, such as *The Working Actors Guide*, published by Aaron Blake, *The Ross Reports*, and *The Illinois Production Guide*, which list agencies. SAG and AFTRA have lists of agencies as well. For information on fit modeling, contact the Fashion Institute of Design and Merchandising resource center or San Francisco Fashion Industries. Call and ask for the directory that lists manufacturers.

A final note: Be wary of any agency that insists on your using a specific photographer or enrolling in expensive classes. It may be getting a kickback.

Good luck.

- **BENEFITS:** Good money for relatively short hours; meeting people; variety of work.
- **PITFALLS:** Strong competition; unsteady income.
- **SOURCES:** Call agencies. Drop off pictures. Go to open calls. Yellow pages under "Designers—Apparel" and "Theatrical" and "Modeling" agencies. *The Working Actors Guide*, published by Aaron Blake, www.workingactors. com. *Ross Reports*, 1515 Broadway, New York, NY 10036. *The Illinois Production Guide*, www.filmillinois.state.il.us. SAG, www.sag.org. AFTRA, www.aftra.org.
- **NEEDS:** Good grooming; positive attitude; portfolio; zed card.

Pharmaceutical Sales Rep

Pharmaceutical sales reps, otherwise known as detail people, visit doctors' offices with specific product samples and "detail" the doctors about the product, hoping for their commitment to try it and pass it along to patients. Doctors are usually open to trying new and improved products for their patients' benefit. As a result, both the doctor and you get to attend the many functions offered by pharmaceutical companies, including black-tie affairs and free educational programs. One of the drawbacks of this job is all the detailed paperwork that needs to be filled since you are dealing in pharmaceuticals.

Good organization and a professional appearance are a must. As with any sales position, it is important not to take the rejection personally when sometimes doctors will give you the brush-off. Sales experience is preferred. Once hired, you have to attend training programs on pharmaceuticals, which typically last a few weeks.

A growing number of pharmaceutical companies now offer part-time positions, often called job-sharing or working mothers programs. For employment leads, go to the library, and research the top pharmaceutical companies anywhere in the country. Look up addresses, and send in your résumé. Another way to procure employment is to ask doctors about pharmaceutical companies and to speak with some friendly reps who visit their offices. Also, local pharmacists can tell you the names of the top-moving drugs and which companies are distributing them.

Base salary depends on experience. Part-time workers can expect to earn $35,000 to $60,000 a year, including bonus and commissions. Many companies will provide you with a car and full health benefits. A few well-known companies to contact are GlaxoSmithKline, Merck & Co., Abbott, and Bayer.

Good luck.

- **BENEFITS:** Flexible hours; part-time programs available; good salary; pharmaceutical company functions.
- **PITFALLS:** Competitive market; a lot of paperwork to fill out.
- **SOURCES:** Doctors' offices. Pharmacists. Pharmaceutical companies. GlaxoSmithKline, 888-825-5249, www.gsk.com.

Merck & Co., 800-422-9675, www.merck.com. Abbott, 800-222-6883, www.abbott.com. Bayer, 203-937-2000, www.bayer.com.

- **NEEDS:** Organizational skills; professional appearance and attitude; self-motivation; background in sales.

Trade Shows and Conventions

At this very moment, not far from you, there is probably a trade show going on. Trade shows, usually held in convention centers, promote such products as computers and other electronics, food, and toys, to name a few. There are conventions held for all types of businesses and products. At McCormick Place (a major convention center in Chicago), conventions include the National Restaurant Association, the Chicago Gift Show, and National Manufacturing Week. For some of these conventions, 250 people a day need to be hired!

Models, actors, students, semiretired folks, and outgoing, friendly individuals are employed to present or demonstrate products in their best light. Other available types of position include convention registration assistants, who help register companies that are displaying their products, retailers, distributors, and consumers. A large number of cashiers, security guards, and room models (people to hand out materials) are needed. Preshow work may include stuffing envelopes, assembling display booths, organizing books and gifts, telemarketing, and acting as an ambassador to the host city.

Scheduling is flexible, depending on when the show is on. You can always decline work, and it won't affect future employment. A typical show can employ you for one day or two weeks, and different shifts, including weekend work, are available. Some shows go from 6:30 A.M. to 10:00 P.M. Wages vary greatly depending on skills, talent, experience, type of show and location, and the client. On the low end it can be $7 to $8 an hour, but it can range as high as $100 an hour for models, experienced actors, and meeting planners.

For employment opportunities, call the convention bureau in your city. Ask what registration companies hire part-time help for shows. The McCormick Talent Agency presently hires for trade shows in Chicago. A library is also a good place to start looking for promotional work. There you will find a magazine titled *Promo* that lists trade companies in the promotion circuit. It rates the top hundred companies once a year. Trade papers such as *Backstage* often have ads as well.

Good luck.

- **BENEFITS:** Good salary; interaction with people; fun; interesting work.
- **PITFALLS:** Having to stand.
- **SOURCES:** Convention bureau. Library. Trade papers, such as *Backstage*, www.backstage.com. Business directory for corporations that do trade shows. *Promo* magazine, www.promomagazine.com. McCormick Talent Agency, 219-395-9823.
- **NEEDS:** Outgoing, well-groomed, articulate, dependable.

Traffic School Teacher

Comedians, actors, retirees, and other people with outgoing personalities are generally hired to teach traffic school to keep students entertained. For those of you lucky enough never to have experienced traffic school, it is the place where people with traffic violations go in lieu of having the violations appear on their records. Day, evening, and weekend classes are offered. Comedy traffic school is popular in California, Florida, and Texas.

The job involves checking traffic violators in, collecting their tickets, and educating them in a funny, positive, and informative manner. A certificate is presented to each student at the completion of the day's course, an eight-hour day with a lunch break and a few other periods of respite. The fun part is that you are performing in front of a captive audience. If you are a comedian, this is a perfect chance to try out new material.

To be hired, you will need to have an interview and possibly show your stuff in front of others. After being hired, you will have to attend an orientation to learn basic driving rules (maybe you'll even know a few already!), watch a few traffic school classes, and then at the local department of motor vehicles (DMV) get a license, which costs about $30.

A teacher is generally paid $10 to $20 an hour, depending on the level of experience. The scheduling of shifts is flexible. Many traffic schools are listed in the yellow pages under "Traffic Schools" or in the classifieds under "Part-time Work." Improv Traffic School is the number one traffic school in Southern California, with more than eighty locations. It also serves Northern California, Florida, and Texas. Another way to find schools is to call your local traffic courthouse for information.

Good luck.

- **BENEFITS:** Entertaining others.
- **PITFALLS:** A small classroom where no one laughs at your jokes.
- **SOURCES:** Traffic schools listed in yellow pages. Improv Traffic School, 800-888-8526, and 310-286-6773. Classifieds. Local traffic courthouse.
- **NEEDS:** Comedic or acting background; outgoing personality.

Welcome Wagon

If you have an entrepreneurial spirit, you can start your own welcoming service. When I moved into an apartment complex in Los Angeles a number of years ago, I received a welcoming coupon packet in the mail that local businesses had obviously paid for. What a great idea some smart entrepreneur had put into action!

In the old days, when you moved into a new neighborhood or town, the welcome wagon would come by with freshly baked cookies and a warm smile. Cut to the modern-day welcome wagon. This mostly suburban phenomenon is a wonderful idea for new town arrivals as well as businesses that are looking to attract customers. You contract with businesses in the community and then meet with individuals and families moving into the area. Newcomers are given coupons and gifts from local businesses as well as information on community affairs, local policies, Little League, schools, religious organizations, and more.

Generally, businesses are charged a small amount for each newcomer. The more businesses involved, the more profit for you or the company you work for. You will be paid by the business per newcomer you meet, typically $10 to $20 total for each. It is feasible to see five newcomers a day. Obviously some towns have more of a turnover than others. If you choose to work for a company such as Welcome Wagon, it is possible to become a salesperson for it, selling its welcoming business in other towns as well.

You are selling individualized advertisement programs, so this job works best in areas with mom-and-pop stores and individually owned businesses. City hall will provide a list of newcomers if it sees this as a valuable service. Giving people materials on ordinances, licensing information, and voting information makes them more aware and responsible citizens.

For employment, look in the help wanted section of your paper under "Part-time," or call city hall to see if it has welcoming services. Welcome Wagon International in Glen Ellyn, Illinois, can refer you to the branch of welcomers in your area.

Good luck.

- **BENEFITS:** Flexible hours; meeting people; fun.
- **PITFALLS:** Business can be slow if there is not much neighborhood turnover; small businesses are being bought out by chains and foreign companies.
- **SOURCES:** Welcoming services listed in paper. City hall. Welcome Wagon International, 800-779-3526.
- **NEEDS:** Enjoyment in meeting new people; friendly, assertive personality; sales ability to solicit funds from local businesses.

6

If I Only Had a Brain
USE YOUR NOODLE JOBS

Adult Education Teacher

If you are an excellent communicator and can motivate other adults, consider becoming a part-time continuing education teacher. There are any number of interesting classes to teach. A few examples include computer technology, preparing for the GED (high school equivalency exam), art, and automotive mechanics.

The majority of jobs are available at vocational or technical schools or with continuing education programs at high schools and universities. There are also numerous independent adult schools where you can teach—for example, the Learning Annex (found in a number of major cities) or Discover U in Seattle. Requirements vary from state to state and school to school. Some programs require a bachelor's degree and a teaching certificate. Information is available from your state department of education and local school districts. Or contact continuing education programs at community colleges and universities and local adult ed schools. If you want to teach a class that has never been offered before, send in a proposal to the program coordinator. Class schedules are flexible. Many classes meet in the evenings and on weekends.

Salary varies widely, depending on where you teach, how many hours you teach, and what you teach. If you have a product to sell, such as a book or handout, you can earn more money. For information on listings in your area, contact the American Association for Adult and Continuing Education in Washington, D.C. This association has a membership department that provides a newsletter, publications, annual conferences, and other networking opportunities. Members are put on a list that goes out to educators. The membership fee starts at about $75.

Good luck.

- **BENEFITS:** Scheduling flexibility; reward of teaching others.
- **PITFALLS:** Work can be sporadic.
- **SOURCES:** State education departments. American Association for Adult and Continuing Education, 1200 Nineteenth Street, NW, Suite 300, Washington, DC 20036, 202-429-5131, www.aaace.org. Local community colleges and adult ed programs. Learning Annex: San Francisco, 415-788-5500; San Diego, 619-544-9700; Los Angeles, 310-478-6677; New York, 212-371-0280; Toronto, 416-964-0011. Discover U is in Seattle at 206-443-0447.
- **NEEDS:** Knowledge of subject; excellent communication and motivating skills; sometimes a degree or teaching certificate.

Book Reader

You don't have to be Evelyn Wood to earn money reading books. If you enjoy reading and have a flair for writing, you can earn money as a freelance book reader at home. Literary agencies and production companies hire book readers to see if certain books would make good films, TV shows, or MOWs (movies of the week).

The difference between being a book reader and a script reader (chapter 3) is that book readers make more money with the reading part. This is an especially good job for a novelist to learn what works and doesn't work and for stay-at-home moms or dads who are afraid their brains are going to mush cooing with their infants. Since you work at home, you create your own hours as long as you meet the deadlines.

To be a book reader, you will need to learn how to do coverage and have to have access to a typewriter or computer. Coverage is a report of approximately five double-spaced pages. The first section (two pages) consists of the cover sheet and a log line that sums up the book in one or two sentences. The next few pages include a synopsis of the book and your opinion on whether it can be successfully transformed into the film or TV medium. After this, you hit the three basics in further detail—plot, story line, and character—and occasionally talk about the setting. Finally there is one page of character breakdown.

It is best to find someone who already does this to show you how the finished product looks. A background in English and writing is preferred, and owning a computer or typewriter is essential. Most major cities offer courses at adult ed schools and community colleges on how to write coverage. Call agencies and production companies, explain why you are an excellent candidate for the job, and ask for a way to get in the door. Expect to earn $85 to $120 for the first 250 to 300 pages read and 8 cents to 20 cents per page after.

There is a great need for book readers in such major cities as Los Angeles, New York, Chicago, and London. There are a number of books to assist you, including *Reading for a Living,* by T. L. Katahn; *Writer's Guide to Book Editors, Publishers, and Literary Agents,* by Jeff Herman; *The Illinois Production Guide,* and *The Hollywood Creative Directory.*

Good luck.

- **BENEFITS:** Working at home; being your own boss; stimulating work; enhances vocabulary, spelling, and speed of reading.
- **PITFALLS:** Reading boring books.
- **SOURCES:** Literary agencies and production companies. *Reading for a Living,* by T. L. Katahn; *Writer's Guide to Book Editors, Publishers, and Literary Agents,* by Jeff Herman; *LA 411* by D. Goldblatt. *The Illinois Production Guide,* 312-814-3600. *The Hollywood Creative Directory.*
- **NEEDS:** Enjoyment of reading; knowing how to do coverage; a typewriter or computer.

Computer Skills Teacher

If you love computers, understand how they work, and keep up-to-date on the latest popular software programs, this may be the perfect job for you. Computers are becoming increasingly ubiquitous in daily life: Using their computers, people pay their bills, balance their checkbooks, shop, create CDs, and print photographs. Many people, however, are still unfamiliar with computers and looking for instruction in how to take advantage of these new electronic options.

For work as a computer skills teacher, you can teach individuals or groups. Most of the time a teacher of groups will work at some kind of learning center, and a teacher of individuals will go to the client's home. When deciding which route to take, know yourself. Do you prefer structure and stability? If you do, working at a learning center is the better choice. If flexibility is desirable, and one-on-one teaching sounds more appealing, you should pursue private lessons. In both cases, you will need to be able to explain properly to your students the basics of how the computer works and how to operate different programs. Teachers often specialize in either PCs or MACs. When you create your business cards or flyers, you might want to mention whether you focus on one or know both. You can also mention any special expertise or familiarity you have with specific types of programs, such as graphic design or financial software

To find a job at a learning center, check the yellow pages under "Schools," or contact local community colleges and adult education centers. Private schools don't have the state requirements that public schools have for teachers, so you might want to look into positions at middle schools and high schools in your area. If this sounds suitable for you, two resources are the Computer Learning Foundation and the National Association of Independent Schools (NAIS). The Computer Learning Foundation is a nonprofit organization geared toward the education of young people. The NAIS has a comprehensive, national list of private schools that are potential workplaces.

Working privately, you can charge $50 to $75 per hour. For private clients, post flyers on community boards, which you can find at supermarkets, churches and temples, and community centers, such as the YMCA. Placing ads in various classifieds is another good way to get your name out. Craigslist is an example of a free, popular, on-line classified listing. I know one teacher who placed a free ad in her community newspaper and found clients that way. The free services are the best way to start. You can generally get all the clients you need (and more) just through flyers, word of mouth, and free classifieds.

Private clients may request that you set up their computer, install new software, and teach them how to use it. It is not necessary to know every program to do this. Many software programs come with tutorials, and you could go through them with your client or on your own. Clients may want you to do anything from setting them up for on-line bill paying or showing them how to burn CDs. Patience and good interpersonal skills are the keys to working privately. If you get irritated when someone asks you the same question five times, teaching one-on-one may not be for you. If, on the other hand, you have the patience to work with novices and don't mind getting back to basics, you'll be all set.

Good luck.

- **BENEFITS:** Learning as you teach; making contacts; little to no initial investment; potential for substantial income.
- **PITFALLS:** Unsteady income until regular clientele is established.
- **SOURCES:** Call institutions about teaching requirements. Check the yellow pages under "Schools." Craigslist, www.craigslist.org. Computer Learning Foundation, Palo Alto, California, 408-720-8898, www.computerlearning.org. National Association of Independent Schools (NAIS), Washington, D.C., 202-973-9700, www.nais.org.
- **NEEDS:** Patience; good communication skills; computer knowledge; more patience.

Creating Web Pages

These days it seems as if Web addresses are everywhere, from magazine ads and billboards to junk mail. Using the Web for promotional purposes is as common as handing out a business card. As a programmer on the World Wide Web you act as the cyberworld version of an advertising agency. Instead of creating an ad campaign for print or TV, you are designing eye-catching Web sites for companies on the Internet.

The process of creating Web sites includes everything from researching customers to writing the code to designing and maintaining the site. You take your clients' company literature and catalogs and translate them into viewable programming on the Web. It is always important to have your clients select some existing sites they like so that you can understand their taste before beginning.

Sam's Teach Yourself Web Publishing with HTML & XHTML in

21 Days, by Laura Lemay and Rafe Colburn, is a good way to acquaint yourself with the process, as is *The Complete Idiots' Guide to Creating a Web Page*, by Paul McFedries. There are plenty of support groups, such as the HTML Writers Guild, which has more than forty thousand members. For additional help, using a search engine, type in "beginning Web design" or "Web authoring." The book *The Internet for Dummies*, by John Levine et al., can be helpful.

To get started, you will need an Internet service provider, an ISP, in Net lingo. There are plenty of ads for providers in newspapers, or you can ask around for recommendations. You can get a dial-up connection, DSL or cable modem. DSL and cable modems are many times faster than dial-ups, but also significantly more expensive. A DSL line is usually set up through your local phone company, and there are often special deals if you use the company for other services. Likewise, cable modems are usually leased through your cable company, but this service is still not available in many areas. A dial-up will be enough to get started but will require more patience on your part. You'll also need a computer with at least 16MB, but preferably 32MB or 64MB, RAM, a fifteen-inch monitor, at least a 56kbps modem, plenty of available disk space, and a graphics accelerator card. If you are uncertain, check the minimum requirements of the browser you will be using—for example, Netscape 7.0. If you want your own domain, speak to your ISP, or contact www.internic.com and fill out an on-line application. Many ISPs offer free Web space with an account. You'll need a Web browser, which is software that lets you view Web pages. Two popular browsers are Netscape Navigator (www.netscape.com) and Microsoft's Internet Explorer (www.microsoft.com). To add graphics, you'll need a paint program such as Adobe Photoshop.

To find clients, spread the word among friends and family, offering discounts or a few free sites in order to practice. Call up business owners or anyone who has a marketing idea and ask if they are interested in advertising on the Internet. For example, contact all the hair salons in your area, and tell them why it would be beneficial to advertise on the Web. One idea is to create a site for all businesses in a certain location, similar to creating a "mall" on the Internet. Expect to earn $500 to $1,500 for setting up and creating the Web site. When you start out, it may take you longer than anticipated to complete a site. Once you begin to build a clientele, however, you can reuse programming. Another way to earn money is to host a site, rent to others, and charge monthly for space on your server.

If you want to work for an established company that creates Web sites, put your name and résumé on the Internet so companies searching for employees can find you. It goes without saying that the best advertisement for yourself is to create your own amazing Web site!

Plenty of courses will help you learn more about this dynamic field. For information, contact independent learning schools, adult ed programs, and local colleges.

Good luck.

- **BENEFITS:** Working out of your home; large earning potential.
- **PITFALLS:** Initial investment for equipment; challenge of learning HTML; being stuck in cyberspace for the rest of your life!
- **SOURCES:** Local colleges. Adult ed programs. Independent learning programs. Books: *Sam's Teach Yourself Web Publishing with HTML & XHTML in 21 Days,* by Laura Lemay and Rafe Colburn; *The Complete Idiots' Guide to Creating a Web Page,* by Paul McFedries; *Internet for Dummies,* by John Levine et al. Try local bookstores or Amazon.com. HTML Writers Guild, www.hwg.org.

- **NEEDS:** Computer, modem, Internet service provider, Adobe Photoshop, Web browser, and Internet knowledge.

English as a Second Language Teacher

To teach English as a second language (ESL) or EFL (English as a foreign language) or ESOL (English to speakers of other languages), it is often necessary to be fluent in a second language. The list of languages needed in the public school system is endless and includes Spanish, Japanese, Korean, and Russian. Knowledge of phonetics is also helpful. There are many opportunities to teach ESL full-time or as a substitute in bilingual elementary and secondary schools, adult education programs, private schools, and private tutoring sessions outside the classroom.

Requirements for teaching ESL differ within each district, so you'll need to contact your state education department or school district's teacher recruitment office for details. For example, to teach in the Los Angeles Unified School District, you need a B.A., credentials in ESL or a fifth year in student teaching, and a passing score on the CBEST (California basic educational skills test). In New York you need to be state-certified to teach in the public school system.

Salary varies, depending on the city. The beginning salary at public schools, for teaching four to five classes a day, is about $27,000 to $35,000 a year plus benefits. Substitute teachers make about $100 to $140 a day. If you teach for more than ten days at one school, the pay generally increases.

Private school requirements vary because they are not under state regulations. If you have ESL experience or are fluent in a language, getting a job at a private institution can be less complicated than at a public school. Check the schools in your area for information on their ESL programs. Look in the yellow pages under "Language Schools" for further listings. Pay tends to be lower at private institutions, and classes at diocesan schools can be quite large.

Tutoring ESL is another option. Credentials are not as important, and you can advertise for free on college campuses by posting notices at the resource center, library, and student center and on classroom bulletin boards. My friend is now privately tutoring three ESL students that she obtained by placing just such an ad. You can charge $40 to $65 an hour to teach privately.

Yet another idea is to teach ESL in adult education classes. If you are interested in this approach, contact individual high schools and universities for specific requirements and pay.

Good luck.

- **BENEFITS:** Making a difference in people's lives; good money; health benefits; using your language skills.
- **PITFALLS:** Lengthy process to complete credentials to teach in the public school system.
- **SOURCES:** State or city unified school districts. Adult education divisions in high schools. Yellow pages under "Language Schools." Advertisements. Some common certificates you can obtain are UCLES Celta, TESOL, TEFL certificates. The TESOL certification training program is 130 hours, 888-547-3369, www.tesol.org/careers/, for more information regarding the different trainings. This site gives information about the various training programs available and how to find a job once you have obtained your certificate. I got the following from an article at www.tesol.org/careers/counsel/qualifications.html: "Elementary or secondary school teachers in most states in the United States must have a degree in education with an endorsement or add-on certification in ESL. Certification re-

quirements can be obtained from state departments of education, and may be reciprocal from state to state."

- **NEEDS:** Teaching experience; training in ESL; B.A. or certificate.

Freelance Graphic Designer

When you go into a restaurant, have you ever noticed how the menu is designed to catch your eye and make the restaurant and its food seem appealing? Or the way a book cover and the styling of the type compel you to open the book and start reading? Well, a graphic designer helped make it that way. Graphic designers work on logos, menus, books, catalogs, Web pages, magazines, and a variety of other print media. Even if you can't draw with a pen or pencil, but still know what you like and have an eye for style, you can find work in this lucrative, abundant field. The computer is your main tool, so you don't have to be able to draw a perfect line.

To get started, you will need some basic computer knowledge and familiarity with basic design principles. Classes are offered through community colleges and extension courses. Trade schools, like Platt College in California, which has a one-year program, will gear you for the field and offer guaranteed job placement. For design programs, contact specific design schools listed in the yellow pages. Most community colleges offer courses as well.

As a graphic designer you can work out of your home if you have a computer and a page layout design program, such as QuarkXPress, Adobe Photoshop, or Adobe Illustrator. Freelance pay is approximately $20 to $75 an hour, depending on whether you work independently or through a temp agency.

If you are working independently, word of mouth is the best way to gather assignments. Be bold with your self-promotion. If you think a restaurant's menu needs a new look, offer your services for a fair price. Take out ads in writers' magazines (see "Freelance Writer," this chapter) or trade publications and community papers. If you are interested in book design, contact editors or designers at publishing houses; they often use graphic design freelancers. For more corporate work, check out trade magazines, such as *Adweek* and *Brandweek*, for available work, or place your own advertisement. You'll also find that many temp agencies are interested in your skills; one nationwide company to contact is Aquent.

Good luck.

- **BENEFITS:** Flexible hours; being your own boss; creative challenges; good wages.
- **PITFALLS:** Independent work can be sporadic.
- **SOURCES:** Community colleges and adult ed programs. Trade magazines. Temp agencies. Aquent, 877-2AQUENT, www.aquent.com. *Adweek*, www.adweek.com. *Brandweek*, www.brandweek.com.
- **NEEDS:** Computer skills; creativity; some design training.

Freelance Illustrator

If you have a background in graphic or fine arts, consider becoming a freelance illustrator. An illustrator creates, draws, and paints a picture, photographs it, and then, using a design program, puts it on the computer. You will need a computer and a few popular programs, which can include Adobe Photoshop, Adobe Illustrator, and Fractal Painter. If you are interested in the entertainment industry, you can find work doing storyboards or production illustrations. Creating the art for children's books and publications is another popular field.

For information on classes that will teach you popular design programs, contact local community colleges and adult ed schools. If you're just starting out, it's a good idea to join a design company, advertising agency, or postproduction house in a junior position, doing storyboard and sketch design. Several people I interviewed agreed that it was better for them to work at a company as an intern or apprentice instead of paying for classes. This way you learn a variety of skills and make industry contacts, and many times the company you're working for will eventually offer you a paid position.

In addition to a résumé, you need an impressive portfolio that contains your best work. Contact advertising agencies and facilities where there is ongoing production for TV, film, and commercials. The library and theatrical bookstores will have books on production companies in your area as well as on illustrating children's books. A few popular ones are *The Illinois Production Guide*, 312-814-3600; *The Hollywood Creative Directory*; *The Working Actors Guide*, published by Aaron Blake; *How to Write & Illustrate Children's Books and Get Them Published*, by Treld Bicknell and Felicity Trotman; and *Children's Writers and Illustrators Market*, published by Writer's Digest Books. For design programs, contact specific design schools listed in the yellow pages. Most community colleges offer courses as well.

Earnings will vary according to your level of experience and the project. As a freelancer you can choose to charge per week, day, hour, or project. You can expect to earn anywhere from $12 to $100 an hour.

Good luck.

- **BENEFITS:** Illustrators are in demand for freelance work with a number of companies; fair amount of artistic freedom; possibility of earning quite a lot of money.
- **PITFALLS:** Your illustrations may not make it to final edit.
- **SOURCES:** Advertising agencies. Graphic departments of

TV stations, film studios, design companies. *How to Write & Illustrate Children's Books*, by Treld Bicknell and Felicity Trotman. *Children's Writers and Illustrators Market*, published by Writer's Market Digest Books. *LA 411*, by D. Goldblatt. *The Illinois Production Guide*, 312-814-3600. *The Hollywood Creative Directory. The Working Actors Guide*, by Mani Flattery.

- **NEEDS:** Artistic and design talent; portfolio; computer; computer programs; and knowledge of software.

Freelance Writer

Freelance writing allows writers the luxury of pursuing their interests while paying their bills. Magazines are ideal places to submit your work, for there are hundreds aimed at every audience imaginable. Writing a few regular articles a month can put food on the table and leave you time to write your magnum opus.

Nonfiction magazine editors look for short feature articles covering specialized topics. The best pieces are geared toward current events of national interest. If you're not an expert, become one through research. Fiction editors generally prefer to receive complete short story manuscripts. It is extremely important to be familiar with your target magazines before submitting your work because editors want to know that you understand their magazine's audience and focus. Always first contact the editor by phone to make sure you understand submission requirements.

Order subscriptions to *Folio* and *Writer's Digest* to keep abreast of what's going on in the publishing world. *Writer's Digest* also publishes a wide range of books for writers, such as *Making Money Freelance Writing. The Handbook for Freelance Writing*, by Michael Perry, is another good resource, as is *The Lit-*

erary Marketplace, one of the most widely used reference books in the publishing industry. It lists every major publisher, publicity outlet, and supplier. Any large branch library will have these books and many others to assist you.

For further information and a listing of more than a thousand magazines in subject categories, I highly recommend *Writer's Market,* published by Writer's Digest Books. You might also consider joining the National Writers Union (NWU), which provides resource materials, seminars, newsletters, and contract advisers. Before you submit your material, you will need to have it copyrighted. Go to the Writers Guild of America in your area, or write to the Registrar of Copyrights, Library of Congress, Washington, DC 20559, 202-707-3000, or visit www. loc.gov/copyright. Pay will vary from approximately $50 to $400 per article.

Good luck.

- **BENEFITS:** Rewarding work; doing what you love; creative outlet; freelance opportunities.
- **PITFALLS:** Unsteady income.
- **SOURCES:** *Folio,* 800-975-5536, www.foliomag.com. *Writer's Digest,* 800-289-0963, www.writersdigest.com. *Making Money Freelance Writing; The Handbook for Freelance Writing,* by Michael Perry; *The Literary Marketplace; Writer's Market,* published by Writer's Digest Books, 800-289-0963. Writers Guild of America, 800-548-4532, www. wga.org. U.S. Copyright Office, 202-707-3000. National Writers Union in New York, 212-254-0279, or access the Web site at www.nwu.org.
- **NEEDS:** Writing ability; creative ideas.
- **IDEAS:** If you enjoy traveling, consider writing and selling your travel experiences. Check out *The Travel Writer's Handbook,* by Louise Purwin Zobel. Try local bookstores or Amazon.com.

Language Trainer

Whether it involves interpreting, translating, or teaching, language training is the perfect job for anyone with a foreign language skill. Interpreters generally translate the spoken word simultaneously on plant tours, at conferences, and at other important events. Translating is written work and can be done from home with a fax machine or a computer and modem. Teaching is done on site at companies or foreign language schools.

Individuals and businesses usually contact foreign language schools for business or travel purposes, although sometimes individuals want to learn a new language just for fun. Two well-known language schools are Inlingua and Berlitz. Inlingua has more than three hundred schools worldwide, with thirty-three in the United States. Each school is a separately owned business that uses the company's teaching methods, materials, and support. The main focus is on business professionals. All employees need to be native speakers or must have achieved a native-level proficiency in their language. All teaching is done in the native tongue, so you do not need to be fluent in English. Prior teaching skills are not a prerequisite, since Inlingua has a specific training procedure and philosophy. Teachers work anywhere from five to thirty-five hours a week. If you are interested in translation or interpreter work, you don't need to live in the city of the school you work for. Materials are faxed to translators, and interpreters can be sent across the country, depending on the client's need. Translators and interpreters usually find work in the legal system.

Attention to detail, grammar, and syntax and an understanding of the culture are important. Phone interviews are accepted. These jobs are freelance and can last a few days to a few months or more, depending on the client's needs. Pay varies. Teachers typically earn $12 to $20 per forty-five-minute class session.

Translators usually earn 12 cents to 20 cents a word with a set minimum, and interpreters $15 to $30 an hour, depending on experience.

For employment opportunities, look in the yellow pages under "Language Schools." The headquarters of Inlingua in the United States is in New York City. To find the closest location to you, go to www.inlingua.com. Berlitz has been around since 1878 and has more than sixty schools in the United States and Canada, with headquarters in Princeton, New Jersey. Call the school in your area, or visit the Web site at www.berlitz.com. Besides offering translation and instruction courses, Berlitz publishes language tapes.

Good luck.

- **BENEFITS:** Meeting people of different nationalities; using your language skills.
- **PITFALLS:** Depending on where you live, there may not be a strong demand for the language you speak.
- **SOURCES:** Yellow pages under "Language Schools." Visit Inlingua at www.inlingua.com or Berlitz at www.berlitz.com, or check the yellow pages to locate the school nearest you.
- **NEEDS:** Foreign language skills, native-fluent; education and business background preferred.

Paralegal

A paralegal is often employed directly by a law firm but can also do freelance work as an independent contractor. The job involves completing government, bankruptcy, and simple divorce forms and dealing with wills, trusts, and miscellaneous court documents. Essentially, you are to a lawyer what a nurse is to a doctor: invaluable.

If you choose to work for a law office, duties may include gathering preliminary information on cases prior to the attorney's meeting with the client. The hours are flexible, and often you will be given a key to the firm's offices and can complete your work when you wish. If you prefer to work independently, you will need to secure your own clients by advertising. You can place ads in newspapers and even paper flyers on cars at courthouses in your region.

I highly recommend taking a course in the fundamentals of paralegal work to familiarize yourself with the required duties and give yourself an edge in the job market. Many private institutions and continuing education programs offer paralegal courses. It is preferable to take a course approved by the American Bar Association (ABA). The Service Center for the ABA in Chicago can provide you with a list of accredited schools in your area. Tuition for a four- to eight-month program at these private institutions is approximately $4,000 to $5,000, and day and evening classes are offered. In Los Angeles, UCLA and the University of West L.A. offer paralegal training, and in New York, Adelphi University and New York University's continuing education program offer accredited courses. For less expensive classes (not accredited by the ABA), look in the yellow pages under "Paralegal" and "Legal" or in the classifieds under "Education/Training" and "Paralegal." Another way of becoming a paralegal is to take a less skilled job, such as a girl/guy friday, in a small law office and then keep taking on more tasks. Also note that some law firms will teach you to become a paralegal.

If you prefer the stability of working for a lawyer or a law firm, you can expect to make $10 to $25 an hour, depending on your level of experience. If you are working independently, the going rate is approximately $300 to $500 per task. Once the work becomes familiar, it takes only about thirty minutes to fill out the forms. For specific jobs, check legal newspapers, such as the *Daily Journal* or *New York Law Journal,* and the classifieds under "Temp Work," "Paralegal," and "Legal." You can also contact law firms directly by looking in the yellow pages under "Attorney."

Good luck.

- **BENEFITS:** Good wages; steady employment; flexible hours; good introduction to law.
- **PITFALLS:** Tedious, detailed work.
- **SOURCES:** Legal newspapers. Classifieds under "Temp Work," "Paralegal," and "Legal." American Bar Association, 312-988-5522 or 800-285-2221, www.abanet.org. Adelphi University, 212-965-8340, www.adelphi.edu. New York University's continuing and professional education program, 800-FIND NYU, www.scps.nyu.edu. UCLA, 310-825-4321, www.ucla.edu, or UCLA Extension, 310-825-9971, www.uclaextension.org. University of West L.A., 310-342-5200. Yellow pages under "Paralegal" and "Legal" or in classifieds under "Education/Training" and "Paralegal."
- **NEEDS:** Knowledge of legal forms; paralegal course.

Princeton Review or Kaplan Teacher

Teaching and monitoring practice tests for the Princeton Review or Kaplan is a terrific part-time job for anyone who has excelled and scored well on a standardized test. Many people are employed by these companies part-time. These organizations prep for the SAT, LSAT, GRE, MCAT, and GMAT, and special courses in each exam are conducted around the country. It is your job to teach students how to recognize what the tests are asking and to prep them in specific areas before the exam date.

To qualify for employment by the Princeton Review or

Kaplan, you must have very strong test scores on the exam you are interested in teaching and excellent skills as an instructor. The ability to deliver information in a way that is entertaining and easy to understand is very important. The pay is $15 to $30 an hour, depending on your teaching experience. Typically you are hired to work seven to fourteen hours a week, and you can always rack up more hours by subbing for other teachers. Each class runs for about three to four hours, and weekend work is available. Upon hiring, Princeton Review and Kaplan both provide training. You will need to send a résumé and cover letter to the grad director or SAT director.

Good luck.

- **BENEFITS:** Good hourly wage; improving your communication skills.
- **PITFALLS:** Driving to different locations to teach.
- **SOURCES:** Call the Princeton Review, 800-2-REVIEW, www.princetonreview.com, or Kaplan, 888-KAPLAN2, www.jobs.kaplan.com.
- **NEEDS:** Above-average test scores; teaching skills; fun and energetic personality.

Private Tutor

If you enjoy teaching on a one-on-one basis, private tutoring may be a great part-time job for you. To be a private tutor, you need to be proficient in a particular subject or language or skilled in a general area, such as teaching children to read. You must be a good communicator who can assess and respond to specific problems, be encouraging, and help make learning fun. Among the advantages of being a tutor are flexible hours, intellectual and emotional stimulation, and good wages. It is a challenging job that enables you to be a mentor while helping another person gain skills and confidence. It can also be extremely demanding; working with children who have poor concentration calls for patience and dedication.

Most clients and tutoring agencies will prefer that you have a bachelor's degree, but it is not always necessary. If you live in California, it is a good idea to take the California Basic Educational Skills Test (CBEST) so that you can put it on your résumé. Call the department of education in your state regarding similar requirements. If you decide you need a little educational backup, a bookstore or library will have plenty of information to enhance your knowledge of the subject you are interested in teaching. Tutoring typically pays $25 to $65 an hour, depending on your experience and whether you choose to go through an agency.

Getting tutoring jobs can be quite easy. Most schools have bulletin boards or job boards, and college and local newspapers often list employment opportunities. Substitute teaching can be a great segue into tutoring because your principal and the school staff will be able to give you references. You may also want to place an ad in your community, church, or temple newsletter. If you decide to go through an established company, the yellow pages under "Tutoring" lists services that you can call for employment.

Good luck.

- **BENEFITS:** Good hourly wage; intellectual and emotional stimulation.
- **PITFALLS:** Working with a "challenging" (politically correct for "irritating") child.
- **SOURCES:** Yellow pages under "Tutoring" for agency listings. College newspapers. Craigslist, www.craigslist.org. Placing an ad in your community, church, or temple newsletter.
- **NEEDS:** Proficiency in a subject or a technique.

Proofreader

A freelance proofreader checks manuscripts and documents for spelling, grammar, and punctuation mistakes. Many writers and English teachers proofread as a side job. Publishing houses and law firms are two major sources of employment. Law firms employ proofreaders to check briefs, wills, trusts, arguments for court, and brochures for legal seminars; publishers hire proofreaders to check manuscripts before they are sent off to the printer.

To get started, you need to take a course in editing or proofreading. Most community colleges or adult ed programs offer classes. Your local bookstore or library will have a number of useful books, such as *Copyediting: A Practical Guide*, by Karen Judd. Before you are hired, you will have to take a basic English grammar test and demonstrate your knowledge of proofreading symbols. Publishing houses will usually require you to own a copy of the style manual they use. *The Chicago Manual of Style*, published by the University of Chicago Press, is generally regarded as the definitive writing reference work. Salary usually ranges from $12 to $25 an hour. It can be on the lower end if you go through a temp agency. Hours vary according to the projects you work on and the deadlines you are given.

To seek proofreading employment, call well-established, large law firms, or send your résumé to editors at publishing companies. For law firms, look in the yellow pages under "Legal Services" and in the classifieds under "Proofreading," "Editing," or "Legal." The trade magazine *Publishers Weekly* lists publishing houses and has a classified section, as do many writer magazines. Corporate newsletters and professional trade journals (American Bar Association, American Medical Association, etc.) are yet other sources to contact. The book *Writer's Market*, published by Writer's Digest Books, is an invaluable resource as well.

Another alternative is to freelance through temp agencies. For a listing, check the yellow pages under "Employment Agencies." I often tell people who are seeking temp work to go directly to the source, to call law firms or publishing houses in your area and ask which temp agencies they use. United Temps is a California-based employment agency serving over a hundred cities nationwide, and the Affiliates Temp is an international company with over 170 offices in the United States and Canada. Its headquarters is in Menlo Park, California.

Good luck.

- **BENEFITS:** Good salary; flexible hours.
- **PITFALLS:** Tedious work.
- **SOURCES:** Temp agencies. Major law firms; professional trade journals; publishing houses. Classifieds under "Proofreading," "Editing," and "Legal." *Publishers Weekly*. *Writer's Market*, published by Writer's Digest Books, 800-289-0963. *Copyediting: A Practical Guide*, by Karen Judd. United Temps, 408-272-8293. Core Staff: Chicago, 312-578-9100, New York 212-557-6252, www.corestaff.com. Affiliates Temp, 800-870-8367, www.affiliates.com.
- **NEEDS:** Proficient English language and proofreading skills; ability to work on a deadline.

Reviewer

A reviewer, otherwise known as a critic, examines a subject of interest (films, books, restaurants, plays, music, dance, or art) and reports on it for different publications. Many writers are also freelance reviewers or food critics; reviewing provides a steady writing gig while you are working on the great American novel or screenplay. If you are a film or performing arts critic, you'll be invited to attend premieres and openings of shows with a guest (your popularity will immediately increase), and if you're a food critic, you will frequent the best restaurants in town.

Qualifications include a strong awareness of current events and in-depth knowledge of the industry you choose to write about. The ability to articulate your views on paper is essential. I suggest that to gain experience as a reviewer, you contact community newsletters and local papers that usually hire almost anybody at extremely low salaries. This way you can develop a solid collection of clips that are representative of your best writing. Also, study popular reviewers to see how their pieces are structured.

Once you have several reviews in your portfolio and have had a few gigs to put on your résumé, find magazines and newspapers that you are interested in writing for, and send a copy of your material (a tear sheet) for the editors to review. In your submission, detail your particular expertise on the subject matter. After you have given editors a chance to look over your submission, follow up with phone calls to get feedback.

This job is flexible because you usually have a week to turn in the article after you have attended the function to be reviewed. Pay varies, depending on the publication and your experience. The going rate is usually anywhere from $40 to $500 an article, often according to the length. *Writer's Market*, published by Writer's Digest Books, updated yearly and sold in most bookstores, provides a price chart for freelance projects.

Good luck.

- **BENEFITS:** Flexible hours; free entertainment or food for you and a guest; use of your communication and writing skills.
- **PITFALLS:** Tedious projects; bad meals.
- **SOURCES:** *Writer's Market*, published by Writer's Digest Books, 800-289-0963. Magazines and newspapers of interest.

- **NEEDS:** Strong writing ability; practical knowledge or expertise in a specific field.

Seasonal Tax Accountant

Becoming a licensed accountant and working out of your home during tax return months will allow you to make a lot of money in a short period of time. H&R Block, a worldwide tax preparation company with about ten thousand offices, offers eleven- to thirteen-week courses in tax accounting that cost approximately $250 to $350. It offers basic, intermediate, and advanced courses. Each state has different tax laws and policies, and you will need to be knowledgeable about those governing your state. In many cities, after you complete the course, you will need to pass a licensing exam. For more information, call the H&R Block in your area, or check other listings in the yellow pages under "Tax Preparation Services."

It is customary to charge between $100 and $250 to complete a basic tax return. This process usually takes about two to three hours and can be done at your convenience within certain time restrictions. Your busiest time will be from the end of March through April 15. A good way to make sure you're not bombarded in early April is to offer discount incentives to people who file their returns before the mad tax season rush.

When going into business for yourself, you need to build a clientele. The money is not steady, but you will make much more per hour than if you work for someone else. To build your private client base, offer free financial advice and planning seminars, at which time you can distribute your business cards. If you choose to work for an established firm, check the classifieds under "Accounting." Many temp agencies hire accountants. ProStaff, with headquarters in Chicago and Minneapolis, is a national employment agency that hires accountants.

Good luck.

- **BENEFITS:** Flexible hours; great hourly wage; working at home.
- **PITFALLS:** Need to market your skills; wages vary.
- **SOURCES:** Yellow pages under "Tax Preparation Services." H&R Block, 800-TAX–7733, www.hrblock.com. Classifieds under "Accounting." Referrals. Give seminars; advertise. Register with employment agencies. ProStaff, 800-938-WORK, www.prostaff.com.
- **NEEDS:** A tax preparer certificate or license.

Substitute Teacher

Being a teacher can be extremely rewarding if you enjoy working with children. Substitute teaching comes with all the rewards and offers flexibility since you can choose when to work. A typical workday is 8:00 A.M. to 3:00 P.M., with a lunch break and a free forty-five- to sixty-minute period.

Different cities have different requirements for teachers. Call your unified school district, educational department, or a local school for specific information. Salary depends on where you live. In most major cities you can expect to earn $110 to $150 a day. Another possibility is to substitute in private schools, which you can contact individually for specific requirements. Primarily they look at your résumé and what you have to contribute. Since there are fewer children per class, the environment is often less demanding, and it is easier to create good relationships with students and the people in charge. Generally you are responsible for only three to four classes a day. The pay at private schools is usually less than at public schools.

Good luck.

- **BENEFITS:** Making a difference with children; good salary; short day; choosing when you want to work.
- **PITFALLS:** Day starts early; disruptive kids.

- **SOURCES:** Yellow pages for private schools. School district recruitment office.
- **NEEDS:** Résumé and interview for private school; B.A., local exam, references from other school districts for public schools.

Temporary Legal Assistant/Lawyer

Perhaps you went to law school but have since moved on to another profession. Well, you can make your degree useful (and your parents happy) by working as a legal temp. If you don't have a law degree but have a legal background and experience, consider being a legal assistant or litigation secretary. Legal temp work is simply a more specialized type of temping and calls for more specific skills. This means you will be paid about double the salary of a standard temp position.

Previous experience with lawyers and the court system and computer literacy are necessities. You must be up-to-date on computer software and proficient in a variety of programs. The ability to prepare the requisite forms and a knowledge of court rules in all counties are mandatory.

When applying for legal work at a temp agency, you may be tested on typing, computer programs, knowledge of legal documents and litigation, and basic grammar and spelling. To learn how to be a legal assistant, you can contact community colleges and private colleges in your area. Many continuing education programs provide classes. Or call your state bar association for course information. Part-time legal temp assistants typically earn $15 to $35 an hour, depending on skills and level of experience. Freelance lawyers charge $100 to $300 an hour, depending on location, size of firm, and specialty.

There are a number of ways to secure legal assistant work. Most states and some cities have their own law periodicals with employment sections, such as the *Daily Journal* in Los Angeles, the *New York Law Journal*, and the *Connecticut Law Tribune*. You can also call lawyers and law firms directly and ask if they are looking for temporary help. This will enable you to make more money since you will have cut out the employment agency. Check the classifieds under "Law" and "Legal" or the yellow pages under "Employment Agencies."

Good luck.

- **BENEFITS:** Good salary; learning about the law; using your law degree.
- **PITFALLS:** Demanding work.
- **SOURCES:** State bar association. Local legal periodicals. *Martindale Hubbell Legal Directory.* Temp agencies. *Daily Journal,* 213-229-5300, www.dailyjournal.com. Visit www.law.com, 800-628-1160, for job openings. *National Law Journal,* 800-274-2893, www.nlj.com.
- **NEEDS:** Legal background; computer proficiency; professional appearance.

Temp Work

Temp work is one of the fastest-growing industries in the nation. It allows companies to hire individuals without providing benefits, a major cost saving for corporations. Temp positions vary, from clerical duties, word processing, receptionist work, bookkeeping, and general office jobs to customer service, accounting, and light industrial and technical positions.

Temping is a great way to gain knowledge about different businesses and make contacts in your specific area of interest. The job stress is fairly low since you have less responsibility than a full-time employee. On the downside, learning each new office routine can be tedious. Most temp agencies offer free training for different computer programs and phone systems and will place you in either long- or short-term assignments. If you desire, many part-time temp positions can turn into full-time (and full-salaried!) work. Wages vary depending on the agency, your experience, and your skills. A receptionist, for example, earns $7 to $14 an hour, whereas computer and word processing positions typically pay $12 to $20 an hour.

When applying for a job, you will be required to take quite a few tests, on spelling, typing, math, and computer skills, depending on the desired position. Many temp agencies offer employment, and I recommend you sign up with several agencies if you want steady work. Check the yellow pages under "Employment Agencies." The large chains have a number of offices, so you can choose the one most convenient for you. If you have a particular area of interest, such as working in a bank, call banks in your area to find out what temporary agencies they work with. Kelly Services and ProStaff are two of the largest and most reputable temp agencies, employing thousands of workers nationwide. Force One Entertainment is New York–based and services the arts, entertainment, communication, and education industries, working with the most prestigious companies in the world.

Good luck.

- **BENEFITS:** Variety of work; making contacts; meeting people; free training.
- **PITFALLS:** Adapting to a new environment; can feel corporate.
- **SOURCES:** Yellow pages under "Employment Agencies." Kelly Services, 248-362-4444, www.kellyservices.com. ProStaff, 800-938-WORK, www.prostaff.com. Force One Entertainment, 212-922-9898, http://forceoneentertainment. com.
- **NEEDS:** The more skills you have, the more money you can make.

3-D Animator

How many times did your kid drag you to see *Toy Story*? All the images in that movie were created by computers. Today cutting-edge animation like the kind used in *Toy Story* is being done in most major cities. Many sculptors and traditional fine artists with computer proficiency who need freelance, part-time work have made the transition into this new medium.

Most people who get into 3-D animation have extremely high computer skills or are 2-D graphic artists already familiar with programs like Adobe Photoshop or QuarkXPress. Three-D falls into two categories: 3-D for PC and Mac and 3-D for Silicon Graphics, Inc. (SGI). Three-D for SGI is the more complex and highly valuable skill to have; thus the pay is higher.

To see if this job would be of interest, take a class at a community college or university, which typically costs $100 or more. Another option is to call one of the major providers of 3-D software, such as Alias/Wavefront, which offers intensive training programs all across the country. After developing some skills, ask your teacher which are the largest animation houses in your area to contact for possible jobs or internships.

You can also search the Internet for employment opportunities. Www.vgyellowpages.com is the yellow pages of video games, www.vsearch.com provides information on companies and jobs, and two job placement boards are www.monster.com and www.jobbankusa.com. *The Hollywood Creative Directory* has a list of interactive and new media companies. Also, every major production company has an interactive division. For example, Disney has Imagineering and Sony has Imageworks. They specialize in new media and animated films. Pay depends on skill and experience. Full-time animators I've spoken with earn anywhere from $35,000 to $75,000 annually, based on their skill and experience.

Good luck.

- **BENEFITS:** Being on the cutting edge of technology; creative outlet; plentiful work; great pay.
- **PITFALLS:** Courses to learn 3-D animation are expensive; finding a 3-D package to learn on can be challenging; takes training to become proficient.
- **SOURCES:** Call your local college or community center for available courses. *The Hollywood Creative Directory,* 800-815-0503 for mail order, www.hcdonline.com. Check the Internet for job placement boards. Alias/Wavefront, 800-451-3318, www.aliaswavefront.com.
- **NEEDS:** Highly developed computer skills; 2-D graphic skills; familiarity with Adobe Photoshop or QuarkXPress.

7

You Gotta Have Heart

GOOD KARMA JOBS

Braille Transcriber

Today many children who are blind or visually challenged are mainstreamed into regular public schools. They use special braille books transcribed for them, which follow the course work. If you are bored with the typical word processing job or are looking for a part-time (or full-time) way to make money from home, this could be an ideal way to assist others and earn a good paycheck.

A braille transcriber uses a specific braille writer or computer with software that translates braille. To be considered for this job, you must be certified by the Library of Congress, which will provide you with a correspondence course and exam. There is no charge to take the course, which is paid for by your hard-earned tax dollars. Many adult education programs offer classes to assist you with the course work. Call local high schools and junior colleges for information.

Pay varies, because certain school districts are more intelligently budgeted than others. A braille transcriber can expect to earn $12 to $25 an hour. The wage usually depends on the level of skill used. Literary transcribers deal with a straightforward format, while textbook transcribers work with columns, charts, and tables. Math transcribers are the most technically proficient, having to work with different codes and symbols.

For employment opportunities, contact your local school district or the city, county, or state board of education. Also try looking in the yellow pages under "Blind Institutions" and "Youth Organizations" for specific organizations for the blind. Good luck.

- **BENEFITS:** Challenging, interesting work, providing a much-needed service; often able to create your own work schedule.
- **PITFALLS:** Deadlines can be stressful; wages can be low because of funding problems in public education.
- **SOURCES:** Local school district. State board of education. Library of Congress, 800-424-8567. Yellow pages under "Blind Institutions" and "Youth Organizations."
- **NEEDS:** Certification from the Library of Congress; word processing skills.

Child Care

It goes without saying that child care requires a love of children. And I don't mean the kind of "I love kids" appreciation when you see them in a park for a few minutes. We're talking hours here. If you really love children, this can be one of the most rewarding jobs in the book. Duties may include picking a child up from school or an after-school activity, meal preparation, overseeing homework assignments, or simply staying with the child while parents are out. The joy of this job is that you are providing a needed service while being a positive influence in a child's life. When you are working at night and the children are sleeping, your time is your own to write, read, study, or watch TV.

Child care usually pays $7 to $15 an hour, depending on the

employer, your experience, and how many children you are caring for. Most child care services require you to have prior experience working with children. You may also need to have a car and car insurance. Many agencies offer twenty-four-hour-a-day care, so there is plenty of shift flexibility. The agency will assign you to specific jobs depending on your experience and shift interest.

For a listing of agencies, look in the yellow pages under "Baby-Sitters" and "Employment Agencies" or in the classifieds under "Domestic Care," "Housekeeper," and "Nanny." Agencies are almost always open to interviewing high-quality people. You will need to fill out an application, have an interview, supply references, and usually submit to a background check. Many health clubs now provide child care, as do a number of churches and temples. If they don't provide it presently, offer to organize it!

If you are good at self-promotion, you can gather your own clientele by advertising or by word of mouth. You can design a flyer or postcard with a personal recommendation from someone you know or have worked for. Offer to baby-sit once or twice for your rabbi's or pastor's children or for any store owner or manager who has a regular newsletter in exchange for a personal recommendation. Places to advertise your services might include community or school bulletin boards, Lamaze classes, pediatricians' offices, prenatal and postnatal classes, and parent magazines. Working in a day care center or at a child care center in a health club, church, or temple can get you more independent baby-sitting jobs. You may even decide to join with one or two other people and start your own child care service or referral agency.

Good luck.

- **BENEFITS:** Working with children; flexible hours; free time when children are asleep.

- **PITFALLS:** Building a clientele if it's your own business.
- **SOURCES:** Yellow pages under "Baby-Sitters" and "Employment Agencies—Domestic Help." Classifieds under "Domestic Care." Advertising: college bulletin boards; health clubs; temples or churches.
- **NEEDS:** Love of children; experience; patience.

Children's Entertainment

Dressing up and entertaining at kids' parties can be a creative, fun way to earn money on weekends. The instant feedback and laughter from children will give you a high unlike any other. Party services look for spontaneous, energetic men and women who enjoy working with children in a party atmosphere. You may be hired to be any number of characters: Batman, a Ninja Turtle, a Power Ranger, Barney, Elmo, or Santa Claus. Many companies will have you create your own character or clown. The hiring company usually provides instructions on the most popular children's games and magic tricks, including that old favorite, balloon animals. This is the perfect job for anyone looking to improve improvisational skills.

If you possess an entrepreneurial spirit, another idea is to create your own children's entertainment company. Two actors I know formed Send in the Clowns. They bought clown costumes, made impressive business cards, advertised, and performed popular children's games and party antics. Soon they had a thriving business and hired a number of employees.

Magic tricks, games, balloons, a pump, and a few costumes are good investments if you are interested in starting your own company. Plenty of books will provide you with fun skits, games, and activities. Costume rentals are also an option for specific occasions or theme parties. Check the yellow pages under "Costumes" for a store near you. To publicize your business, donate your time at city events that are listed in the newspapers, and then hand out your business cards. Volunteering your time at a few birthday parties in exchange for referrals is also a great way to get started. Advertise in local parent magazines and community papers, and put up signs at pediatricians' offices. The classified sections of local magazines have listings of party services.

Before starting your own business, work for an established children's entertainment company to learn the ropes. Such companies look to hire creative, fun, upbeat, and imaginative individuals who enjoy working with children. They are listed in the yellow pages under "Entertainers" or in parent or local magazines. Most party services and agencies will pay you $30 to $75 an hour plus tips. Unfortunately, most parties employ you for only an hour, so you may need to do quite a few weekend gigs to make a decent weekly wage. When it is your own company, you can charge $100 or more per hour and do the gig yourself or hire it out.

Another related way to entertain children and earn money is to work as a face painter. You don't even need to be that artistic; you can paint really simple designs on kids' faces. A woman I know painted faces at the Microsoft picnic (twelve thousand attendees!), as well as for Nordstrom and Bon Marché. She worked through an agency (look in the yellow pages and classifieds under "Entertainment" and "Talent Agency") and earned $25 to $35 an hour in Minneapolis and $20 an hour in Seattle. You can also go it alone and paint faces at fairs and festivals.

Good luck.

- **BENEFITS:** Weekend work; creative outlet; fun; good hourly wage.
- **PITFALLS:** Being pulled over by a cop while wearing your purple dinosaur costume!

- **SOURCES:** Yellow pages under "Entertainers." When starting your own business, advertise in local parent magazines and community papers; put up signs at pediatricians' offices.
- **NEEDS:** Enjoy entertaining children; improvisational skills.

CPR Instructor

Teaching a course in CPR allows you to earn money while passing on knowledge that can save lives. Everyone should know CPR. Teachers, foster parents, M.D.'s, aerobics instructors, health care providers, security officers, police officers, sheriffs, dentists, and firefighters are some of the people required to be certified in CPR.

Some basic teaching skills are necessary, as well as certification through the American Heart Association or the Red Cross. The Red Cross, for example, offers a course to become First Aid/CPR/AED Instructor. The course runs about twenty-five to thirty-five hours, costs about $165, and is usually completed in four to seven days. The Red Cross will also require that you take its short introductory course titled "Fundamentals of Instructor Training," which is about five hours long and costs $25. Once you are an instructor affiliated with a training center, you will be able to give out CPR cards and your training center will process paperwork.

Each city is different in its teaching methods. To find out more about affiliated training centers in your city, call the American Heart Association. For information on the American Red Cross, contact the office in your area. When you have completed all requirements and become certified, you are on the roster of the American Red Cross. It will refer clients to you and act as an authorized provider. To find work independently, establish a relationship with pediatricians who will then recommend you; advertise at birthing classes and prenatal and postnatal exercise classes and in local community papers and newsletters. Salary varies, depending on experience and where you teach. Hospitals and the Red Cross have different policies on payment. Private teachers typically charge about $50 to $75 per client.

Good luck.

- **BENEFITS:** Helping people learn to save lives.
- **PITFALLS:** Need to be recertified periodically, which involves a review session and a recertification fee.
- **SOURCES:** American Heart Association, 800-AHA–USA1, www.americanheart.org. To find the American Red Cross in your area, call 877-272-7337, or call the national headquarters, 202-737-8300, www.redcross.org.
- **NEEDS:** Ability to instruct others; certification in CPR instruction.

Doula

The moment when a child is born is truly a miracle. You can take part in this life-changing experience by becoming a doula and assisting women during and after childbirth. A friend of mine compared childbirth to running a marathon in terms of endurance and pain. (I did both, and childbirth is infinitely more challenging!) A doula offers the old-fashioned community care that used to be prevalent and that mothers deserve.

Doulas are not trained midwives, though during births they provide invaluable emotional support and nonmedical pain relief. In addition to the nurturing and coaching aspect, doulas assist in preserving the memory of the birth experience for the family. Often they will provide a written account of the entire birth for the parents. As a doula you will have to be the most relaxed person in the room. If you are a birthing doula, you may have to be on call for as long as two days. Usually there is a minimum of two prenatal meetings to connect and build up trust with the mom.

A postpartum doula is hired to take care of the mother at home. This includes helping the mom rest by taking charge of other responsibilities as well as assisting with breast-feeding and the needs of other children in the family. It is important for a doula to fit comfortably in other people's homes and not take up a lot of space or be overbearing in any way. Having a child is often a difficult transition for families, and sensitivity to the situation as well as to what needs to be done is crucial. A postpartum doula is usually hired for anywhere from a few days to six weeks, determined by the family.

Wages vary. Experienced doulas in major cities typically earn $15 to $25 an hour. Childbirth doulas work on a sliding scale, charging about $300 to $1,000 a birth. To be trained as a doula, contact a midwifery center or doula center in your area. The American College of Nurse Midwives is in Washington, D.C., and the Midwifery Education and Accreditation Council is in Arizona. Look in local parent magazines and newspapers as well as in the yellow pages under "Birth Centers." There are also a number of doula organizations across the country. Doulas of North America, known as DONA, in Seattle, trains and certifies doulas nationwide, offering two- to three-day workshops. The cost varies widely, depending on whether food and accommodations are included. Some workshops have cost anywhere from $50 to $300. It takes approximately six months to two years to become certified. DONA requires you to attend its workshop, to be present at three births, and to write an essay on what you've learned at the births. You need a good evaluation from the parents as well as an attending caretaker (doctor or midwife). The certification packet costs $35, and membership in DONA costs $40 per year.

To get work as a doula, you can advertise at maternity stores, prenatal exercise classes, and childbirth classes as well as in child care referral books and parent newspapers. You should also network with medical professionals and doula organizations.

Good luck.

- **BENEFITS:** Participating in the miracle of birth, rewarding on a personal and spiritual level.
- **PITFALLS:** Being on call; work can be exhausting; earnings are unsteady.
- **SOURCES:** Advertise at maternity stores and in child care referral books and parent newspapers. Network with medical professionals and doula organizations. For training, contact the American College of Nurse Midwives, 202-728-9860, www.acnm.org; Midwifery Education Accreditation Council, 928-214-0997, www.meacschools.org; and Doulas of North America, 888-788-DONA, www.dona.org. Check yellow pages under "Birth Centers."
- **NEEDS:** Energy; patience; faith in natural processes; calmness; being comfortable in other people's houses.

Pet Care

Pet care is a terrific job for animal lovers since you are around pets on a steady basis. While owners are working late hours or traveling, they need a responsible person to take care of their beloved four-legged companions. This is where a dependable pet service comes in.

A pet care service can involve dog training, dog walking, cat-sitting, boarding pets, grooming, and more. Payment and schedule flexibility vary, depending on whether you operate your own business or work for an established pet care service. Pet care can be full-time or part-time employment. The jobs I have chosen to focus on are pet-sitter, dog trainer, and mobile pet grooming.

PET-SITTER

Pet-sitting requires the least amount of training and experience of all pet care jobs. It can involve dog walking, pet feeding, litter box cleaning, house visits, day care, sleep-overs, boarding, and trips to the vet or groomer. A pet-sitter can be self-employed or work at an established center like Best Friends Pet Resorts & Salons. If you are hired at an established center, you take care of the animals there and are usually paid an hourly rate. Check in the yellow pages under "Pet Sitting" for possible employers. Best Friends Pet Resorts & Salons has centers nationwide and offers private doggy playtime sessions, and "doggy day camp."

If you are self-employed, the hours are more flexible. Self-employed pet-sitters offer single-dog walks, group walks, doggy play groups, and boarding. Self-employed pet-sitters will either board the animals at their own houses or stay at their clients' homes. For daytime dog walks, most owners give you a two-hour range—for example, a walk between 1:00 P.M. and 3:00 P.M. There is a downside to pet care, though. Pooper-scooping and cleaning litter boxes can be unpleasant (especially when it's not for your own "darling" pet).

Payment depends on whether you operate your own business or work for an established pet care service. A typical visit is twenty to forty minutes, and $10 to $20 per visit is the going rate. The more extras (trips to the vet or groomer, caring for more than one pet, administering medicine), the more chargeable time you have. House-sitting or boarding generally runs from $20 to $50 a night per dog. It varies according to the amount of time the owner wants you to spend with his/her pet, your location, and whether the dog is high maintenance or not. A dog-sitter I know regularly charges $30 per night and gives 15 to 25 per cent off a second dog, depending on the circumstances.

When I was just out of college, I decided to combine my love of animals with my entrepreneurial spirit and start my own pet care service. From day one I began earning money and found it a fulfilling and lucrative side business. To get started, I simply made up a catchy flyer and introduced myself to dog-walking neighbors and pet owners at nearby parks. I even placed flyers on neighborhood cars. I made up a cute business card and introduced myself to nearby pet stores and vets. Soon I had a thriving enterprise and was charging $15 a walk and $40 to $50 for boarding (only two doggies at a time since I lived in an apartment!) with no overhead. I found that for a small business, it was most profitable to stick to the immediate area to minimize traveling time.

To get a business license, which costs about $100 to $150 a year, call your city's tax and permit division or county clerk's office. The National Association of Professional Pet Sitters is a nonprofit organization that provides group rates for liability insurance and bonding. It offers a toll-free referral line, mentor programs, conventions, and regional meetings. The cost of membership is $160 a year, and there are more than a thousand members nationwide. For further information, contact the main office in Washington, D.C. To work for an established pet care service, check the yellow pages or your neighborhood pet store, or call the National Association of Professional Pet Sitters for services in your area.

Good luck.

- **BENEFITS:** Being around animals; self-employment; flexible hours.

- **PITFALLS:** Pooper-scooping; irregular income.
- **SOURCES:** Yellow pages under "Pet-Sitting." Pet stores and dog parks. Neighborhood markets. Newspaper ads and pet magazines. National Association of Professional Pet Sitters, 800-296-7387, www.petsitters.org. Best Friends Pet Resorts & Salons, 203-846-3360, www.bestfriendspetcare. com. Your city's tax and permit division or county clerk's office.
- **NEEDS:** Sense of responsibility; love of animals; license and bonding if you're an independent entrepreneur.

DOG TRAINER

If you don't already have experience dog training, you will need to attend dog training seminars and workshops. Many are relatively inexpensive, approximately $30 to $50 per day. The American Dog Trainers Network recommends at least twenty-four one- to four-day seminars or workshops on dog-related subjects. It lists subjects that should be covered on its Web site, www.inch.com/~dogs/protrainer.html. The Association of Pet Dog Trainers has a list of workshops and seminars, which you can find on its Web site under "Training Events."

This isn't a job you can start overnight if you don't already have a significant amount of experience working with dogs. Getting certified by the National Association of Dog Obedience Instructors (NADOI) is a way you can make sure your knowledge and experience are adequate to start training as well as a good way to promote yourself. NADOI has a list of certified dog trainers available to the public. In total, you should have three to five years of study and dog training practice to become a beginner trainer. Several reputable trainers have warned that many correspondence classes for dog training are expensive and inadequate. If there is one that you are interested in, contact your local Society for the Prevention of Cruelty to Animals (SPCA) or one of the other organizations listed below to find out how creditable it is.

As a dog trainer you can charge $15 to $25 per hour per dog for group lessons; in a group there are usually four to ten dogs. Privately, you can charge about $40 to $60 per session, generally an hour. If you prefer to work at an established center, Best Friends Pet Resorts & Salons hires dog trainers. Check in the yellow pages under "Pet and Dog Training" to find other places for possible employment.

Good luck.

- **BENEFITS:** Being around animals; flexible hours; substantial income; helping people and animals get along better.
- **PITFALLS:** Years of experience and training necessary.
- **SOURCES:** Yellow pages under "Pet and Dog Training." American Dog Trainers Network, www.inch.com/~dogs/protrainer.html. Association of Pet Dog Trainers, 800-PET-DOGS, www.apdt.com. National Association of Dog Obedience Instructors (NADOI), www.nadoi.org. American Society for the Prevention of Cruelty to Animals, 212-876-7700, www.aspca.org. Best Friends Pet Resorts & Salons, 203-846-3360, www.bestfriendspetcare.com.
- **NEEDS:** Love of dogs; experience and education; patience; license and bonding if you're an independent entrepreneur.

MOBILE PET GROOMING

If you just can't get enough of brushing our fuzzy friends and you want to be self-employed, mobile pet grooming is a pet care job that allows you to have a flexible schedule and earn a substantial income with minimal training. Mobile pet groomers generally offer the same services that salon groomers do. Most of the clients for mobile pet groomers are dogs, but cats sometimes require treatment as well. Services that you will be expected to perform as a groomer are nail trimming, ear cleaning, thorough brushing, detangling, and cutting of the hair or fur, flea shampooing, skin and coat conditioning, and teeth brushing. Deodorizing from skunk sprays and other specialty services may also be requested.

Training is necessary, but it is not as long and as arduous as training for other professions. There are many pet grooming institutes across the country that offer reasonably priced programs. Most grooming institutes offer two levels of study, sometimes referred to as the advanced program and the basic program. The Academy of Dog Grooming Arts in the greater Chicago area offers a professional groomer course and a groomer's assistant program. The professional groomer course entails 400 to 500 hours of schooling, costs approximately $4,000, and can be completed in fourteen to twenty-two weeks. The groomer's assistant program is 214 hours, costs approximately $2,500, and can be completed in six to sixteen weeks. Advanced programs run anywhere from 250 to 500 hours of schooling and usually cost between $3,000 and $4,500, while basic courses are about 150 to 250 hours and cost about $2,500. There isn't a national requirement for schooling, so you should find out what is acceptable in your area or where you hope to work. In New York City, check out New York School of Dog Grooming, and in the D.C. area, the Maryland School of Dog Grooming. If you prefer small classes, consider the Southern Institute of Pet Grooming, in South Carolina.

You can charge about $40 to $70 per dog for grooming which will take you an hour, more or less. That is for a basic cut and dry. For other services, such as ear cleaning and nail trimming, you can add $10. Mobile pet groomers charge anywhere from $10 to $30 more than salons.

Certification in Pet First Aid and CPR usually come as part of a grooming program and are important in case anything happens to the pet while it is in your care. Also, it is wise to get insurance. Gibson-Governor Agency, Inc. offers insurance specifically for mobile pet groomers.

You can put together your own mobile unit in a trailer or a van, or you can purchase a predesigned one. A predesigned trailer unit will cost you about $20,000 to $25,000, while a van will cost between $30,000 and $40,000. If you are good with your hands, it may be worth your while to create your own mobile grooming unit. If not, you can buy or lease one premade. Wag'n Tails Mobile Van & Trailer Conversions has vans that you can buy on a finance plan. Ultimate Groomobiles is another source.

Good luck.

- **BENEFITS:** Being around animals; helping pets look their best; flexible hours; substantial income.
- **PITFALLS:** Sometimes the dogs aren't thrilled to be groomed.
- **SOURCES:** Chicago area: Academy of Dog Grooming Arts, 800-333-9034, www.academyofdoggrooming.com. D.C. area: Maryland School of Dog Grooming, 301-585-4311, www.mdschoolofdoggrooming.com. New York City: New York School of Dog Grooming, 212-685-3776, www. nysdg.com. Southern Institute of Pet Grooming, 864-639-6872, www.centralsc.com/sipg. American Society for the Prevention of Cruelty to Animals, 212-876-7700, www. aspca.org. Dog's Outfitter, 800-FOR DOGS, www.dogs outfitter.com. Wag'n Tails Mobile Van & Trailer Conversions, 800-513-0304, www.wagntails.com. Ultimate Groomobiles, Inc., 888-826-5845, http://members.aol. com/groomobile/. Professional Mobile Groomers International, 866-BE MOBILE, www.petgroomer.com/pmgi. htm. National Dog Groomers Association of America, 724-962-2711, www.nationaldoggroomers.com. Gibson-

Governor Agency, Inc., 877-PET GROOMER, www.gibson governor.com.

- **NEEDS:** Love of dogs; patience; insurance; license and bonding if you're an independent entrepreneur.

Professional Companion

With more of the population reaching elderly status, the need for adult companionship is growing. Many adults (or their children) are willing to pay for companionship for different purposes. An elderly person might hire someone to help with such tasks as shopping, preparing meals, and doctor visits or simply to keep him or her company.

To be a companion, you must have patience and compassion and be extremely responsible. If you genuinely care about the people you spend time with, it is both a monetarily and an emotionally rewarding position. It is a great relief for an elderly person to know that on Tuesday from 1:00 P.M. to 4:00 P.M., someone will come over with a car to visit or take him or her to an appointment.

When starting your own business, you will need to obtain a license, which costs approximately $150. Contact your state's department of human resources for elderly care. You may also choose to look into specific car insurance if you plan to transport people for medical reasons. For liability insurance and bonding information, contact a local insurance company. A fair rate for this service is anywhere from $10 to $20 an hour, depending on your skills and your clientele. For example, if you play an instrument, know CPR, and own a car, you may be able to charge more. Some great places to advertise are senior centers, nursing homes, beauty parlors, and local markets and in temple, church, and community newsletters.

Good luck.

- **BENEFITS:** Emotionally rewarding work; new friendships.
- **PITFALLS:** Person may become ill or die.
- **SOURCES:** Religious and community newsletters and senior center bulletins. Nursing homes, beauty parlors, and local markets. Your state's department of human resources for elderly care for licensing.
- **NEEDS:** Patience; sense of responsibility; plenty of TLC to give.

Psychic

Can you sense when an event will take place? Have you been told by others that you possess extraordinary psychic abilities? Well . . . even if you haven't, there are still opportunities for you in this interesting and ever-expanding field. As a psychic you can try to procure work independently or work for an established hot line.

If you do not possess an innate psychic ability, you can learn tarot cards, playing cards, or the I Ching (the ancient Chinese Book of Changes, considered one of the oldest and most reliable tools for divination). There are scores of books on these subjects in bookstores and libraries, often in the metaphysical, occult, and New Age sections. New Age magazines often have advertisements for courses in astrology and tarot card reading. Practice doing readings on friends until you have the process memorized. If you choose to work for a hot line, you will be tested over the phone before being hired.

What's especially beneficial about working for a hot line is that you can work from anywhere (including Canada). You are given a number and a code to dial on your home phone, which then hooks up to the psychic company's line. It provides you with an extension, although you will need to have a line without call waiting.

This job is flexible since you sign up for times when it is convenient for you to work. Expect to work a minimum of sixteen to twenty hours a week. Wages vary, depending on experience, but you can expect to earn about 40 cents a minute and 10 percent of the sales, which amount to roughly $7 to $12 an hour. Regulations presently cut off calls at twenty minutes. Some companies pay an hourly rate plus a commission, while others pay just a commission. There are always new companies entering this field. Commercials on your cable TV stations will provide numbers (unfortunately, you probably will have to pay for the first minute), and you can call seeking a number for employment. Three popular companies to work for are the Psychic Friends Network, the Psychic Readers Network, and the American Association of Professional Psychics. Some companies, such as the Psychic Friends Network, require a number of years of experience.

Many psychics also earn money working out of their homes and at private functions. Building a clientele usually results from word of mouth. Try advertising in local papers and magazines or offering your services for free at parties or as a side attraction in restaurants. You can even put out a sign and sit in the street or in a park like a traditional Gypsy fortune teller.

Good luck.

- **BENEFITS:** Working at home; flexible hours; assisting people.
- **PITFALLS:** Sporadic work if you're on your own; unsteady income.
- **SOURCES:** Contacting hot lines. Advertising. Psychic Friends Network, 800-797-4477, www.psychicfriendsnetwork.net. Psychic Readers Network, 800-742-8309. American Association of Professional Psychics, 800-815-8003, www.certifiedpsychics.com.

• **NEEDS:** Psychic ability or knowledge of tarot cards, astrology, or I Ching.

Rebirther

Imagine a gentle process that can rejuvenate the body and heal the mind and spirit, and all you have to do is breathe. Yoga masters and martial artists have known about the power of breath to heal and transform for centuries. The process is called rebirthing. Through rebirthing, one becomes more aware of thoughts and patterns that may prevent one from living life to the fullest. Using conscious breathing and affirmations (an affirmation is a technique that immerses new thoughts into the consciousness), you release negative thought patterns affecting your behavior. The process empowers practitioners to participate in their own self-healing.

To become a rebirther, you must first go through the rebirthing process. No professional credentials are necessary, but a number of training centers and individuals that will train you are listed in New Age magazines. Dr. Eve Jones, the director of Rebirth Associates in Los Angeles, conducts training and workshops throughout the country, as do many other rebirthers. Training is $300 for an individual session or a four- to five-hour workshop. Upon completion of training, determined by you and your rebirther, you may go into business for yourself, generally through word of mouth. Try advertising in local health papers and magazines or putting up flyers at gyms, health food stores, and centers for alternative medicine or therapy. Rebirthers generally charge from $60 to $120 per session, with sessions lasting anywhere from forty-five minutes to two hours. A number of centers throughout the country teach rebirthing, and there is an Association of Rebirthers and Trainers.

Good luck.

- **BENEFITS:** Control over your own hours; healing and therapeutic work; good wages.
- **PITFALLS:** Lack of public awareness; criticism and skepticism; building clientele.
- **SOURCES:** Health papers and magazines. Rebirthing centers. Philadelphia Rebirthing Center, 1027 Sixty-ninth Avenue, Philadelphia, PA 19126, 215-424-4444, www.philadelphiarebirthing.com. Rebirth Associates of Los Angeles, 323-461-5774, www.rebirthla.com. The New York Rebirthing Center, 212-534-2969 (phone and fax). Association of Rebirthers and Trainers International, Inc., www.artirebirthing.com.
- **NEEDS:** Desire to learn the process; interest in the healing arts.

Social Service

Working for a social service organization is a way both to contribute to society and to support yourself financially. Many social services rely on federal and state funding and therefore often look to volunteers for assistance. However, many flexible, paying part-time jobs are available. Income varies greatly. For a general listing, check your local yellow pages under "Social Services."

A good example of a service organization is the Jay Nolan Community Services in California. This is a wonderful organization whose goal is to keep developmentally disabled people out of institutions. Often Jay Nolan will put them in their own semi-independent private living situations, a community of friends, roommates, and families who foster self-respect, self-care, and growth. Many people with disabilities can function quite well with a little supervision and guidance. That's where you can help.

The two jobs available for people who have not been trained

to care for the disabled are in residential support and relief staff. Residential support means sharing a home with a disabled person. In exchange for being a "friend" and caring for your disabled roommate, you receive a free place to live and a salary of approximately $1,000 a month. The extent of care varies according to the individual's needs. Often it includes doing ordinary activities together, such as shopping, running errands, and going to the movies. It can also include cooking meals, administering medication, and driving the person around. A residential support position allows for plenty of free time, rent-free living, and an income in exchange for your services. Unfortunately, this job means giving up some of your privacy. It requires a gentle, patient, communicative personality. If disabilities make you uncomfortable, this kind of work situation is not for you.

The other position, relief staff, involves "person-sitting" when the primary caregiver needs an evening or weekend off. Pay is about $50 for a five- to six-hour evening, with $8 to $12 for each additional hour and $200 for a weekend live-in situation. This job allows you to be of assistance while retaining your privacy. It is also more flexible; you can set a specific schedule or be on call.

Social service programs differ in their needs and requirements. Contact individual programs for specifications. When you seek employment, you will be screened by a staff member and at least one of the clients for whom you are being considered. Usually a second interview is set up for paperwork to be filled out. You must also commit to taking certain training classes, provided free of charge, which include teaching strategies.

Good luck.

• **BENEFITS:** Helping others; steady salary; challenging work; room and board.

- **PITFALLS:** Loss of privacy; detailed process to be hired.
- **SOURCES:** Yellow pages under "Social Services."
- **NEEDS:** Patience; gentleness; sense of responsibility; communicativeness; desire to help others.

Youth Mentor

These days the media inundate us with stories of abused or neglected children. The job of youth mentor is a very rewarding part-time position that enables those with time and energy to make a significant difference in a child's life. Many family service agencies have mentor programs that are paid positions and are not to be confused with volunteer organizations, such as Big Brothers/Big Sisters. Often they look for people who have backgrounds in psychology, social work, or education. The basic job description includes planning activities and participating with young clients on a one-to-one basis. Wages vary, depending on experience, but you can expect to earn $7 to $15 an hour. Hours depend on your employer's needs as well as your availability.

There are a number of ways to go about contacting family service agencies. Look in the yellow pages under "Family" and "Counseling" (it may refer you to another directory listing), or call the city or county human services department and get a list of nonprofit youth agencies funded in your area. You can also try calling schools and day care programs. Agencies look for people with patience, nurturing personalities, and excellent communication skills. Often a car is required.

Good luck.

- **BENEFITS:** Flexible schedule; variety of activities; opportunity to make a difference in a child's life.
- **PITFALLS:** Highly stressful at times.
- **SOURCES:** Family service agencies. Yellow pages under

"Family" and "Counseling." City or county human services department. Schools and day care programs.

- **NEEDS:** Working well with kids; patience; being a good listener; background in psychology, social work, or education preferred; often a car is required.

ACKNOWLEDGMENTS

Hundreds of people contributed to the production of this book. I am deeply appreciative to all those who wholeheartedly shared their numerous ways of earning money—and their Rolodexes for further interviews! I am filled with gratitude and respect for all of you who have helped advance the idea that there are plenty of part-time, flexible, and even fun ways to earn money.

Special thanks to:

My agent, Simon Green.

My editor at Broadway Books, Ann Campbell, and her assistant, Jenny Cookson.

Danna Katz, who spent many hours assisting me with research and new job ideas.

Sharone Katz Jelden, my dear friend who researched a number of jobs for me, while taking care of her toddler and being pregnant with her second child.

Tara Wilson Doyle and Kim Starzyk for their assistance with many aspects of this book, and, more importantly, for their friendship.

Aunty M for reading first drafts and Uncle Larry for a bounding generosity in creating promotional materials, as well as for their endless support.

My parents, Barbara and Michael Frenkel, for tremendous love and support.

My husband, Jordan Jacobson, my "Be-Sheret" of life for contributing his amazing talents, love, support, and sense of humor to my life on a daily basis.

Our beautiful daughters, Maya and Shira, for adding so much joy to our lives.

Finally, I thank God for my talents and the angels who surround me with so many blessings.

INDEX

Accreditation Council, 216, 217

MMI/America's Best 900#, 44

MobileWorks, 18

modeling, 169–71; artist's, 152–53; fragrance, 162–63

mover, 133–34

Movie Extra Work for Rocket Scientists (Chambers), 102

Mr. Boston's Official Bartending and Party Guide, 56, 61, 65, 85

Mulligan Management, 111

multilevel marketing, 22–24

music: choir work, 98–99; Express, 76; karaoke performer, 106–7; mobile disc jockey, 19–20; pianist for comedy and improv, 113–14; singing telegrams, 116–17; street performer, 117–18; teacher, 21–22; theme park performer, 119–21; varied work, 121–22

Music Teachers National Assn., 21, 22

Music Teachers List, 21, 22

N

National Academy of Sports Medicine, 123, 125, 139, 140

National Apartment Assn., 3

National Assn. of Dog Obedience Instructors, 220, 221

National Assn. of Independent Schools, 182, 183

National Assn. of Professional Organizers, 28, 29

National Assn. of Professional Pet Sitters, 219, 220

National Assn. of Residential Property Managers, 2, 3

National Bartenders School, 61, 65, 85

National Certification Board for Therapeutic Massage, 15, 17

National Cosmetology Assn., 166

National Federation of State High School Associates, 143, 144

National Flea Market Assn., 46

National Flea Marketeer, 46

National Information: Yoga Alliance, 151

National Law Journal, 205

National Research Group, 167

National Sports Performance Assn., 123–24, 125

National Strength and Conditioning Assn., 123, 125, 139, 140

National Writers Union, 192

Natural Epicurean Academy of Culinary Arts, 33

Natural Gourmet Cookery School, 30, 32

Network Telephone Services, 44

New Jersey Casino Control Commission, 57, 58

New York Department of Consumer Affairs, 155, 156

New York Production Guide, 40, 41, 115, 116

900 Know-How (Mastin & Ginsburg), 42, 43

900 numbers, 41–44

O

Om Yoga Center, 151

101 Great Mail-Order Businesses (Hicks), 14

Original Guide to American Cocktails and Drinks, 56, 61, 65, 85

outdoor wilderness and teamwork instructor, 134–36

Outward Bound, 135, 136

P

Pacific Coast Studio Directory, 40, 41

painting houses, 136–38

paralegal, 194–96; schools, 195, 196

party: enhancer, 110–11; promoter, 24–25

Party & Paper Retailer, 5

Party Staff, 60

© PAUL DAVID

ABOUT THE AUTHOR

DEBORAH JACOBSON, a cantor, singer, writer, wife, and mother, has owned and operated two successful part-time businesses. She lives in Stamford, Connecticut.